Cherish

Cherish

NEW AND SELECTED POEMS

Steve Kowit

UNIVERSITY OF TAMPA PRESS

Manufactured in the United States of America
Printed on acid-free paper ∞
First Edition

On the Cover: "Mooring" (detail). 2011. Oil on canvas. 18 x 24 inches.
Copyright © 2015 by Joel Kowit. All rights reserved.
Reproduced by permission of the artist.

The University of Tampa Press
401 West Kennedy Boulevard
Tampa, FL 33606

ISBN 978-159732-127-3 (hbk.)
ISBN 978-159732-126-6 (pbk.)

Browse & order online at
http://utpress.ut.edu

Library of Congress Cataloging-in-Publication Data

Kowit, Steve.
  [Poems. Selections]
  Cherish : new and selected poems / Steve Kowit.
     pages ; cm
  ISBN 978-1-59732-126-6 (pbk : alk. paper) -- ISBN 978-1-59732-127-3 (hbk : alk. paper)
  I. Title.
  PS3561.O87A6 2015
  811'.54--dc23   2015020140

Contents

The First Noble Truth

New Poems

For Mary, my beloved wife, always and everywhere;
in loving memory of my parents;
for my friends, both living & gone;
for the many animal companions who have blessed my life;
for the spirit of Quan Yin, who hears the sufferings of this world;
and for you

And do not call the tortoise unworthy because she is not something else.

Walt Whitman

Lurid Confessions
(1983)

Kind of a Love Poem

Love, this is the cold truth:
there are no centaurs
or druid spirits
or guardian angels.
No tooth fairy, either.
The Baal Shem Tov
is not about to rise from the dead.
Nor is Jesus. Nor is Houdini.
Maybe the Ancient of Days
is a good egg
like the Bible says
but as for the spirit
outlasting the body,
forget it.
Armageddon perhaps,
but the 2nd Coming
is out of the question.
Yet if emotion endures,
then this, the song of our life together,
pressed in an old book
like a dead rose,
might fall,
hundreds of years from now,
into the hands
of some archivist
cataloguing the dark ages,
who'll be shaken
back by the song
to his own life,
& shivering,
feel the presence
of ancient lovers,
if only
for that one afternoon,
centuries after these arms
that wound about each other

are fragments of bone
& our lips dust
& our names forgotten.

Joy to the Fishes

I hiked out to the end of Sunset Cliffs
& climbed the breakwater,
sneakers strung over my shoulder
& a small collection of Zen poems
in my fist.
A minnow
that had sloshed out of someone's bait bucket,
& that I came within an inch of stepping on,
convulsed in agony.
Delighted to assist,
I tossed it back into its ocean:
swirling eddies sucked about the rocks,
white Pythagorean sailboats
in the middle distance.
Kids raced the surf,
a labrador brought down a frisbee,
& the sun sank pendulously
over the Pacific shelf.
I shivered & descended,
slipping the unopened book
into my pocket
& walked south
along the southern California coastline—
all the hills of Ocean Beach
glowing
in the rouged light
of midwinter sunset.
Even now
it pleases me to think
that somewhere
in the western coastal waters off America
that minnow is still swimming.

The Garden

Years ago we owned two cats who hated each other.
When I said we had better give one away
you wouldn't hear of it—you
were adamant, outraged . . .
relenting only weeks later when it was clear
they were going to tear each other to shreds.
I remember the speech you made:
if it came to that we would give away Sluggo,
our lovable calico,
who could purr his way into anyone's heart.
For in less tolerant hands, Mphahlele,
our difficult, misanthropic gray
might be abused, or abandoned . . . or worse—
    whereas
if he lived with us he would be loved always.
& of course you were right,
tho God knows you have paid dearly
for a compassion as absolute
& unyielding
as the copper sheet of the Mexican sky
rising each morning over that house
high in the hills of Chiapas
that you loved so
with its eleven rooms,
those great hanging bells of datura,
that courtyard, tangle
of wild vines
that you would never let me weed
to begin a garden,
insisting in that quiet way of yours
that every creature
had as much right to live as we had,
& that it *was* a garden.

Small Boats

The California tuna fisherman
who bought my van in Puntarenas
had a son who'd been killed in the war.
I remember sitting in the heat & listening.
He was a bald guy with a bulbous nose,
& a talker. He made his
wife bring in Mike's photo.
Then he started in on the Chinese,
how they were going to take over the world.
"William, don't ... please ...
no one's interested ..."
The coffee cup rattled in her fingers.
Afterwards we bused back along the coast road,
a thick fog rolling in off the Pacific
like a Sung scroll:
small boats disappearing in the mist.

Cutting Our Losses

In a downtown San Jose hotel,
exhausted & uptight & almost broke,
we blew 16 *colones* & got stewed on rum.
You lounged in bed
reading *Hermelinda Linda* comics
while I stumbled drunk around the room
complaining
& reciting poems out of an old anthology.
I read that Easter elegy of Yeats
which moved you,
bringing back that friend of yours,
Bob Fishman, who was dead.
You wept. I felt awful.
We killed the bottle, made a blithered
kind of love & fell asleep.
Out in the Costa Rican night
the weasels of the dark held a fiesta
celebrating our safe arrival in their city
& our sound sleep.
We found our Ford Econoline next
morning where we'd left it,
on a side street, but ripped apart
like a piñata, like a tortured bird, wing
window busted in, a door
sprung open on its pins like an astonished beak.
Beloved, everything we lost—our old blues
tapes, the telephoto lens, the Mayan priest,
that ancient Royal Portable I loved,
awoke me to how tentative & delicate
& brief & precious it all is, & was
for that a sort of aphrodisiac—tho bitter
to swallow. That evening,
drunk on loss, I loved you
wildly, with a crazy passion, knowing

as I did, at last, the secret
of your own quietly voluptuous heart—you
who have loved always with a desperation
born as much of sorrow as of lust,
being, I suppose, at once unluckier,
& that much wiser to begin with.

A Vote for Harold

The kid who's taken the paper route for the summer,
a doughy, asthmatic schlemiel
with a blubbery bottom
& bifocals big as moondogs
& cockeyed hair,
hasn't a shot at paperboy of the season
& two weeks in Miami.
For him a good day is passing the schoolyard
without getting punched in the head.
Our block is the worst. He has to pedal uphill
in the wind. You can hear him coming for miles,
straining & wheezing—then a forlorn
little squeal at the crest
like a possum shot from a tree
& a crash that rattles the dishes.
Then, after a silence, his broken,
woebegone voice among the azaleas.
I no longer lunge out of my chair like I used to
but calmly stroll into the yard
& remove the handlebars from his thorax.
He blinks thickly, releasing a sob.
Together we salvage the home edition
that's scattered over the alley—
it too full of mayhem & ill luck:
an air disaster in Argentina,
a family of seven lost in a flood,
the hand of a refugee reaching thru barbed wire,
clutching at nothing, a hand so thin
it will eat anything—straw, dung, wind . . .
& then he is gone, wobbling into the gutter,
that exemplary herald of the Abyss,
dogged on all sides
by curses & screeches & horns,
& is lost in the distance

disheveled, & shaking his head
like a man who is forced to bear witness
to things too awful to mention,
& pedaling like hell.

For My Birthday

Friends, a moment ago, standing here at the table, ready to blow out
the candles, it came to me—if it's true what you say, & I do indeed
seem to grow younger with each passing year, then in no time at all
Mary & I will be back in that Ocean Beach duplex, with its rapture
of white camellias, my vertigo gone & my lower spine supple again,
& my hearing & sight as sharp as ever they'd been.
& Sally & JayJay will still be alive, & Binky & Ivan purring away
on the sofa. Outside, the Pacific pounding the cliffs with its ancient,
millennial music, an exaltation of sea-nymphs,
& surfers bobbing like half-notes out past the breakers: the heart
a blue frisbee spinning over that beach from Pescadero to Brighton.
If you're right & I keep growing younger, I'll find myself
back in the Andes: Esmeraldas. The rains of Tumaco.
The Popayan hills in the misty weeping of dawn.
That thundering gorge into Baños. The road
thru the steaming Peten to Tikal.
                        —It is morning. Chiapas. Your voice
as it was, rising over that rosewood guitar that you loved so,
in that courtyard of wild datura.
McHenry. The Sandias at sunset. The two of us young again
in that railroad flat in the Fillmore, our bodies entwined in the dark.
Cold peaches in moonlight. The Avalon Ballroom. To be with them
again, those who disappeared across borders & oceans,
into anonymous cities, ashrams, communes—Phoenix House,
prison, the Cuetzalan mist. Seen for the last time
on a street in downtown Seattle, Lima, Panajachel: Jeremy . . .
Franklin . . . Gregory . . . Owen . . . Elizabeth back in Manhattan
    Beach—
all that impossible beauty. Death with its hacking cough
& its cryptic shudder, its final ambiguous phonecall. Death
suddenly sitting up in its bed. Death with a spike in the vein,
the husk of the spirit slumped at the wheel of a Buick somewhere
in Tucson. Half a century's streamer of blood in the rain.
The unending immolation of Asia. The cakewalk of black mortification.
cows swinging from hooks, rabbits blinded for one more cream
blusher & lipstick, dogs in terminal agony circling their cages. Isaac

Bashevis Singer was right: for the animals every day is Treblinka.
To be back on the streets again agitating & marching—
What else is there for it?
                    Dearest, if every year I grow younger,
does that mean that someday I'll find myself back in Manhattan
without you? Your name unknown to my lips. Not even to know
you exist, that you stand at the cusp of the future, waiting
for me in its shadows.
                    Beloved, I do not think that I wish to be back there
without you. It's simply out of the question. I absolutely refuse. I . . .
Agh! what am I saying—Nothing will stop it. I'll float thru the Village
with Murray at midnight, past the old Cedar Bar, Les Deux Megots,
the rippled winos of 3rd Avenue curled in their doorways. Past the painted
Ukrainian eggs of the Lower East Side. Past Thompkins Square Park.
That I climb the six flights of that walk-up on Avenue B. All that music
& *mishegas* & metaphysical fervor. Night
lit with its incense & tongues, its muted horn & its velvet drum. Night
with its muffled cries in the dark. O soft-limbed lost girls of my youth,
how purely this time around I will love you.
                    Let it snow again on the Hudson!
Let the sirens wail & the buses belch & the tugs on the East River
sound their guttural honks. Let the poetry readings begin once again
at Le Metro—Ed Sanders & Mickey Ruskin presiding.
Let the streets of Manhattan hum again with its poets & waifs
& musicians & mad action painters, its feverish vanguard of doomed
& beautiful women. Let the Puerto Rican domino players squat on their crates
outside their *bodegas* under the bulging *piñata* of sunlight.
Let their voluptuous daughters promenade thru the streets & their sons
sing five-part harmony in the echo-chambered tenement hallways
of 6th Street. This time around I'll listen more raptly.
This time I'll know what I'm hearing. This time I won't miss a beat.
                    8th Street at Fifth.
McDougal & Bleeker. Mott & Canal. To cross Crane's bridge
out of Brooklyn again—cathedral & harp over the river into downtown
ruckus Manhattan. White buildings lit with the golden palette of morning.
The guts of a disemboweled piano strummed on a vacant street

[15]

in the roseate dawn of the '60s: *Missa Benedicta*
of Avenue C —crescendo of taxis & buses.
Let Cassidy knock again at my door. Let him harangue me once more
with his breathless paean to Mao. Let Rozzie awaken beside me.
Let Lenny regale me with one of his endless apocryphal tales of Bonnard
& Monet as we hoof it back from Penn Station
—Yes, yes, I say. Very true! Absolutely the case!
We are lost in the bright air of impossible gaiety, incomparable youth,
jubilatio of camaraderie, passion & blather: that feast made of fine talk.
Let me wrangle with Jim over Wittgenstein's last proposition.
That's what I want—to yammer all night over that which cannot be said!
Wax ecstatic with Jack on one of those long evening strolls
around Sheepshead Bay—Drunken boats of our Brooklyn boyhoods;
the two of us cooked to the gills on Celine & Rimbaud & Miller
& Crane & Genet.
                    That house on 14th Street.
It's just a matter of time till I'm back there again.
My folks in the doorway—vital & young.
All morning I stand by that maple tree out by the curb, its bronze plaque
announcing that somebody's son had been killed in the War:
just a name & some dates, like this poem: reminder that somebody lived.
To stand dumbstruck with love of a schoolgirl whose name has been
swallowed up by the decades. No matter. Let me return to worship
her image again. Let my mother yak on the phone with my grandmother,
Bertha, impoverished lame widowed immigrant girl of the *shtetls*
of Poland. Listen. You can hear it: the two of them gabbing away together
in Yiddish. Dad in the backyard, laconic & patient, up on that rickety
paint-splattered ladder. He's putting the screens up for summer.
The garden a bliss of roses & mums. How good they both look!
How delighted & young! Just a couple of kids!
I swear it, they've never looked better! happier! younger!
I tell you I can't wait to be back there,
though it's half a century yet down the pike! A curly-haired kid
staring out thru the window at sunset over the backyards of Flatbush,
full of unnamable longing, in love with the burnished light

of late afternoon. The Brighton Express in the distance. That cradle
of wires. The pigeons & sparrows. The rolling past of the clouds.
Unspeakable intimations of what they might mean.
—Birthdays yes, but no such thing as goodbyes. In love,
though I didn't know it then, with the whole inexplicable business.
First sorrow & first wisdom. A mote of molecular dust, like an ant
on a leaf, blown across infinite seas. To be here at all! To have
bubbled up out of the void! Who would have guessed it?
                                        Friends, thank you for coming.
Doesn't the cake look delicious?
For myself, of course, I am absolutely delighted to be here among you.
Immeasurably pleased. Thickening paunch, stiffening joints,
vertigo, bum back, wrecked hearing & sight notwithstanding.
Alive nonetheless! All of us! Here in this strange, unspeakably
marvelous life. & Mary, companion & love, here beside me.
A wish? Friends, what on earth more could I wish for?
Like you say—every year I grow younger. So be it!
Okay, are you ready? Hush now . . . . I'm going to blow out the candles.

Desperate Solutions

For weeks now the parts of a poem,
a scramble of fittings & rivets & gears,
have been clanking around in your head
like the guts of an unassembled machine
till at last, with one jolting image, a gift,
the device you had never been able to find,
everything snaps into place
& you dive for your notebook—
But Jesus, there's never a pen
when you need one: the Scripto blotches,
the Pentel's a leaker, the Flair scrapes like a bone.
In your bottom drawer is a magic marker
that hasn't worked in a decade,
the stub of a pencil, an orange crayola,
& 12 thousand paperclips & erasers.
& digging around in a box on the floor
you karate your head
on the underside of the table
& everything crashes about you
including the coffee
that spills down your shirt.
You shriek as your flesh starts to blister
& that's it! That's all you'll take!
So you hurl the mug at the wall
& snatching a pin from its cushion
you jab it as deep as she'll go
into the tip of your finger.
Then biting your tongue & spitting in pain
you goose it once with your thumb
till a sleek jet spurts from the wound
to the page like a leak sprung in a hose
or the blow of the tiniest whale,
only red. There! Perfect!
As ever, the poem,

which began as a simple machine,
has turned itself into another Rube Goldberg
contraption—a slapstick improvisation
born out of chaos, plucked from disaster,
& written in blood.

Lurid Confessions

One fine morning they move in for the pinch
& snap on the cuffs—just like that.
Turns out they've known all about you for years,
have a file the length of a paddy wagon
with everything—tapes, prints, film—
the whole shmear. Don't ask me how
but they've managed to plug a mike into one of your molars
& know every felonious move & transgression
back to the very beginning, with ektachromes
of your least indiscretion & peccadillo.
Needless to say, you are thrilled,
tho sitting there in the docket
you bogart it, tough as an old tooth—
your jaw set, your sleeves rolled
& three days of stubble . . . only,
when they play it back it looks different:
a life common & loathsome as gum stuck to a chair.
Tedious hours of you picking your nose,
scratching, eating, clipping your toenails . . .
Alone, you look stupid; in public, your rapier
wit is slimy & limp as an old band-aid.
They have thousands of pictures of people around you
stifling yawns. As for sex, a bit
of pathetic groping among the unlovely & luckless:
a dance with everyone making steamy love in the dark
& you alone in a corner eating a pretzel.
You leap to your feet protesting
that's not how it was, they have it all wrong.
But nobody hears you. The bailiff
is snoring, the judge is cleaning his teeth,
the jurors are all wearing glasses with eyes painted open.
The flies have folded their wings & stopped buzzing.
In the end, after huge doses of coffee,
the jury is polled. One after another

they manage to rise to their feet
like narcoleptics in August, sealing your fate:
Innocent . . . innocent . . . innocent . . . Right down the line.
You are carried out screaming.

They Are Looking for Che Guevara

The lecturer writes the phrase *free enterprise* on the board in green chalk.
Above it white pustular fissures appear, which is the strangler
fig taking root in that part of the map devoted to Indonesia.
The metallic pit of the fruit grown from the miracle seed of the green revolution
begins ticking. The peasants dig in. The secret bombing begins.
The porpoise & bison & whooping crane lie down on top of the lecturer's desk
& begin disappearing.
Meanwhile the Huns push on to the Yalu River searching for Che Guevara.
The CIA is hunting for him in the Bolivian Andes.
Ferdinand Marcos & 6,000 Green Berets are hunting for him in the Philippines.
Ian Smith is hunting him down in Zimbabwe.
A small flame appears in the map of Asia:
it is that part they have burnt down searching for Che Guevara,
queen-bee of the revolution.
They are hunting for him in Angola, Korea, Guatemala, the Congo, Brazil, Iran,
Greece, Lebanon, Chile. 9,000 Ozymandian paratroops
drop over Santo Domingo with searchlights, searching for him.
He is not there. He is gone. He is hiding among the Seminoles.
He throws the knife into the treaty with Osceola.
He conspires with Denmark Vesey.
In Port-au-Prince he is with Toussaint.
He reappears later at Harper's Ferry.
He is in Nicaragua, in Cuba where they have embargoed the rain.
The CIA has traced him to Berkeley, but he is in Algeria too
& Uruguay, Spain, Portugal, Guam, Puerto Rico.
Not all the ears of the dead of Asia will lead them to him.
He goes home, embraces his wife, embraces Hildita, embraces the children
of Buenos Aires, gives his compadre Fidel an *abrazo*, lights his pipe,
pours a cup of *maté*, takes a pill for his asthma,
cleans his rifle, reloads it, writes the *First Declaration of Havana*.
Torpedoes of Intergalactic Capital, Inc. blow up the screaming hair of the global
village. B52s drone overhead. It is dawn. They are checking every frontier.
They are looking for Che Guevara.

Conquistador

While his troops looked on from a distance
the President flanked by his aides
stood at the site of the smoldering rubble
where formerly cities had stood.
Shells cratered the fields that remained.
Water, bursting thru shattered dikes,
gushed from a thousand wounds
so that much of what once was the land
was a river, & the river was blood.
All about lay the dead.
"We came in the name of Peace,"
the President cried,
"& the peace has been won!"
Nothing stirred
but the smoke of dead cities
& bubbling mud.
The President opened his fly,
winked at his aides,
& peed
on the bloated corpse of an infant
that lay in the mud.
The conquering army, somewhat dismayed,
pretended not to have seen,
but that night at the victory feast,
after his toast,
a bird,
the color of ashes,
flew out of the President's egg.
& the diplomats looked at their plates
& nobody said a word.

Golden Anniversary

For Michael & Billie Kowit
on the occasion of their 50th wedding anniversary

1.

One night, back home in Brooklyn after 15 years, I sat around with Mary
& the folks going thru the books of their old photos:
pictures of my dad in knickers in his late teens looking rakish
in a t-shirt & sailor cap, holding the center pole of a pup tent—
in his early 20s, hitchhiking to Montreal & drinking from a flask
at the side of a road. Next to that, a piece of birch bark that he sent
my mother from that escapade—postmarked Maine, Sep. 2, 7 a.m, 1926.
My mother with a tennis racket in '27, & smiling from a swimming pool
in '28. They are sitting on the railing of a ship;
my father in a bowtie & knit sweater, she beside him,
a lovely girl of 16, their arms & feet touching.
They're just kids. They look beautiful, both of them, the picture's
dated July 4, 1923. & there's my mother with the Guild Players
in *Disraeli* & there they are at Camp Allegro surrounded
half a century ago by friends who have remained beloved to this day.
& then they're on their honeymoon skating on a frozen lake
out in the woods of Pennsylvania, in the faded sepia gold
of old snapshots—a series of them skating on the ice, holding hands,
my father with a pipe by a pine tree, my mother leaning
on the pillar of the house where they were honeymooning,
hands sunk in her pockets, her face gleaming.
In the last of that series Mickey, my father, has his arms around her,
they stand on the frozen lake, the woods behind them
in their black skates & leather jackets,
he holds her to him, they are radiantly happy, they have
just been married; it is December, 1928. The ancient, black
paper edges of the photo album as I turn the pages
crumble like confetti, & fall like tears.
Beyond the joy & tenderness & passion of these early snapshots,
that are dated in the upper corners, but which time has partially erased,

& against the zeitgeist: all fashion, the grief of history & the drift of the age,
I honor them for the steady burning of their devotion.
May all of us be blessed by love
as faithful & unswerving.
They have been married 50 years.

2.

Dad, one day over 30 years ago you rigged a small sail to an old rowboat
& we set off across a lake high in the Berkshires.
It was the end of summer, a day in August bathed in stillness.
I was a small boy, you a strong, quiet man in your 40s.
Now & then small waves slapped the thick sides under the oarlocks.
Then a wind came up so fast & quietly we hardly noticed it
until it seized us; the small boat tossed about
bobbing like a cork. I grabbed the sides, you worked the sail loose
quickly & unleashed it, & we drifted, oarless, far out,
waving our arms & fruitlessly calling out to the few oblivious
figures on the dock, the sun glinting ominously off those high waves.
Had it come to that we might have swum for the other shore. Summers
before you had taught me: one hand lifting my belly
the other pressing my back—I would kick & kick
holding the rope with both hands, squinting my eyes from the splashing.
Quiet, gentle, efficient, infinitely patient, I think you are more
healer than teacher. In those childhood illnesses,
I would wait hours for your figure to appear out of the shadows
of the hallway; you would enter the room & say "hi, Butch,"
& sit quietly at the edge of the bed,
& it was the same quiet reassurance of your presence

beside me that summer day, bathed in light,
when we were tossed about on the waters together,
which turned what might have become a small boy's panic
into a kind of bliss, that we were stranded
together, alone, drifting . . .

& 30 years later felt the same bliss
when we swam together in the warm waters
off the coast of Miami. Alone with you again I had the same
experience of your gentleness, your quiet grace & strength.
Dad, I think your tolerance & patience for the world
has been my strength for 40 years.
Odd, how little we have ever spoken to each other
& how absolute the love that has bound us.
The distance of a continent means nothing.
We are still together, tho older: a man & his small son
drifting thru a void that is turbulent & calm by turns—
marvelous beyond words, ineffable & exquisite: silent
in a world of absolute stillness
on a lake that is infinite.

3.

Ma, you stand at the dining room table & unfold
a paper napkin & place it, a white, translucent shawl
over your dark hair. Then you light two candles.
It is Friday evening. Outside the light is fading
from the world over Brooklyn, over East 14th Street,
with the darkness of early winter. As the room surrenders
to that darkness your white hands circle the small flames
of the two candles: they thin & flicker under your fingers.
Then you close your eyes & recite the *brocha*.
I can barely hear you. An elevated Brighton Local
rumbles thru the darkness over Kelly Park. The shadow
of your body sways almost imperceptibly against the stairs:
How red your cheeks are in the light

of those two candles. Then the sound of the train
disappears & I hear you sobbing—tears run down your cheeks.
You cover your face with your hands (perhaps
because I am there at your side in the dark room),
but your grief cannot be contained.
Your body trembles.
The candles, that are for the sabbath, & honor the creation,
are also, like the *yertzite* candle burning in the glass in the kitchen,
for the dead. For your mother, Bertha, my grandmother,
who has recently died. & as your grieving shadow sways & sobs
the *brocha*, you have become again that small girl
dancing down Second Avenue more than half a century ago.
You are in a yellow dress, with ruffles,
you are carrying something home, some fish
or fruit wrapped in newspaper, a page from the *Daily Forvitz*,
you are dancing among the pushcarts of Delancey Street,
you are dancing thru the door of the settlement house
& under the impoverished tenement stairways of the east side.
In this family portrait your father's image is dissolving
as you & your brothers & sisters blossom into your own lives.
Now you are married, now the chaos of the Great Depression,
now Mickey graduates from law school, you give birth to a daughter,
& a son. The pitiless war like an evil wind:
your brothers disappear for 4 years. They write from the battlefields
of France. There are tormented, desperate phone calls
in Yiddish. The Jews of Europe are slaughtered.
The screen door of the apartment in Bensonhurst slams shut.
Roosevelt dies. We move in with your mother in the Bronx;
Rosemont catches fire; you buy the house on 14th Street;
Camp Tamarack & the Pines, & the black Plymouth
& college for the kids & Carol's wedding. Your son
kisses you goodbye & flies off to California.
It flickers, all of it, on the wall by the stairs
with your weeping shadow twenty years ago.
As I watch you there, in silence, helpless; not just my mother now,
but a woman, swaying over the sabbath candles

in that most ancient grief,
how my heart embraces you, tho I say nothing. Not a word.
How dark it is & how quiet. We are alone. Dad is dozing in the dark
in the other room. Carol is upstairs with her homework;
the last gray light of the day seeps thru the curtain.
A loaf of challah catches the light. It stands on a silver tray
on a white cloth. The tissue paper shawl on your dark hair
shivers in the flame & glows with its own light.
& then it is done. Your hands withdraw from your face.
The *brocha* ends. & the sobbing.
& when you take off that shawl all the past disappears
into those two, small yellow flames.
I wake Dad up, & standing at the foot of the stairs
yell for Carol to come down to dinner
& now you are taking the roast out of the oven & dad
does his funny cakewalk into the dining room,
that mischievous grin on his face & you say,
"Mick, don't be such a wise guy, please"
& I laugh, & Carol sets the table & I grab a piece of challah
& dad grabs a piece of challah too,
& ma, you tell us to hold our horses & you
complain about having to put the roast back three times
but your face is beaming—your complaint full of joy
& I squeal I have to have gravy, I can't eat anything without gravy,
Carol brings in the potatoes & we're all talking at once,
the mindless yammer of delight about the feast you have prepared
for us so lovingly—with such devotion—
that you have always prepared for us—
& it's great, ma . . . it's absolutely delicious— all these years,
the feast you have made for us all. Ma, it's wonderful
it's absolutely wonderful.

Guests of the Nation

We enter in festive spirits, giggling in the dark
amid a handful of indifferent drunks & empty chairs.
The Jolly Trolley, Christmas Eve. Up front,
two ex-Saigon hookers in stiletto heels,
their bloated breasts bouncing as they stumble
drunkenly about the stage, are fondling themselves
& grinning for the folks who poured the kerosene
& tossed the match & then, astonished
at the conflagration, offered up asylum
to the unincinerated.
Obliviously drunk, & unapproachably tricked out
in that lubricious music, whirling
in a parody of lust, they seem, if anything,
less naked than the rest of us, while in the semi-dark
their huge inflated breasts bear witness to,
if not our generosity, our genius for display
& packaging, & the technology of mutilation:
sliced apart, they have been stuffed
like pillows, or like hunting trophies—
even in this smokey darkness you can see the scars.
& then it's over. The vocalist winds back
into a sexy whisper & the saxophone behind her
sputters like a candle & blows out.
& in that silence, stripped of the bravado of the dance,
how shyly they bow to us, how awkwardly,
& are at last naked & vulnerable.
There is a trickle of applause.
A slot machine in the casino lobby vomits up its nickels
& as in a seamless dream of unaccountable transitions
they are back among us,
in their blouses & black g-strings, grinning
sleepily & hustling drinks, & dumping out the ashtrays:
nothing much, but it's a living—
Christmas Eve, Las Vegas, 1979.
The end of a decade.

Wanted—Sensuous Woman
Who Can Handle 12 Inches of Man

—from an ad in the *Miami Phoenix*

She was sensuous to a fault
& perfectly willing
though somewhat taken aback.
In fact, at first,
she noticed no one at the door at all.
"Down here! . . . down here! . . ."
I shrieked.
—Need I add that once again
I left unsatisfied.

The Rose

Home late, I eat dinner
& read the paper
without noticing
the rose in the yellow
glass on the dining room table—
not until
Mary shows it to me.
"Isn't it lovely?"
"Where'd you get it?"
"A fellow named Bill."
"Oh?"
"Just some guy who comes in
to the bar occasionally . . .
Isn't it lovely?"
"He gave it to you?"
I turn to the editorial page.
"Yes . . .
he just got out of the hospital."
She bends
& takes in its fragrance.
She is wearing that black negligee.
"The hospital?"
She straightens up & looks at me & sighs.
"He's dying of cancer."
We stare at each other.
I want to embrace her,
tell her how much I love her,
how much I have always loved her.
But I don't.
I just sit there.
When she walks back into the bedroom
I see it at last,
glowing on the table,
leaning toward me
on its heartbroken stem.

Raking In

I pull into the driveway.
Mary, in a bright red bandana,
is raking the leaves.
When I left this morning
grosbeaks & chickadees
sat in the feeder but
now nothing sings but the leaves:
life is precious
precious
the dead leaves sing.

I take up the other rake & join in.

These are the leaves
that have lain all winter
under the snow.
They are sodden & faded.
I am careful to rake in
only the dead,
leaving the lovely wild
plum & yellow crocuses
standing—
the first of our flowers to bloom.

Simply that: we are together
raking the lawn,
life is over too soon
too soon
the dead leaves sing.

405

I figured to leave early, drive the coast road,
score a Chinese restaurant, & lay out
by the ocean for a while & get stoned & write
& watch the women, hit the buyers, spend
the afternoon with Bill, catch the sun
sinking over the Pacific, & be home for dinner.
But it didn't pan out: I got off to a late start,
killed an hour in a bookstore,
settled for a Jack-in-the-Box bean burrito.
The beach was out, the buyers weren't in,
the sun went down without me.
Bill & I embraced & parted in a single gesture.
Around midnight, driving back on 405,
it came to me how quickly everything
was passing, & suddenly it was all luminous—
the abacus of lights, the moon, cold
wind whipping thru the window
& myself alive, impermanent . . .
for the eleven millionth time I vowed
to change my life.
A mist came up, the night settled in about me
& I dreamed sweetly of all that I will never become—
women, wisdom, poetry & revolution
disappearing in the purr of the engine & the moan
of the road, & the song of the radio.

Lullaby

—after Atila Josef

Sweet love, everything
closes its eyes now to sleep.
The cat
has stretched out
at the foot of your bed
& the little bug
lays its head
in its arms,
& your jacket
that's draped on the chair:
every button has fallen asleep,
even the poor torn cuff . . .
& your flute
& your paper boat
& the candy bar
snug in its wrapper.
Outside,
the evening is closing its eyes.
Even the hill to the dark
woods
has fallen asleep
on its side
in a quilt of blue snow.

Out of McHenry

Broken fence thru the mist.
Bitter fruit of the wild pear
& vines full of berries.
The stone path
buried in brambles
& mud
& the shack in ruins,
rotted thru
like an old crate:
half the roof caved in.
The whole place
gone to weed & debris.
Someone before me
sick of his life
must have figured this
was as far away as he'd get
& nailed it up
out in the void,
then died here
or left
decades ago.
A swallow
skitters among the beams
& flies out
thru the open frame of a window.
Now nothing inhabits the place
but tin cans
covered with webs,
a mattress,
a handful of tools
busted & useless—
& myself
where he stood
here in the doorway,
in mist,
high up over this world.
Trees & flowers dripping with cold rain.

Home

You arrive in Paradise feverish with anticipation, assuring yourself that everything will be perfect—no migraine headaches, no ambulance sirens, no goodbyes. & it's true: the view from your sitting room is breathtaking, the service impeccable, the food enticingly garnished, & although the water tastes slightly metallic, there is always the coke machine in the lobby. & the climate—the sort of weather you love, one glorious day on the heels of another. You stroll down the beach, under the mangroves & sea grape trees in love, as you were on Earth, with the word *oceano*, white seagulls, the bronzed & half naked women—women who are everything you have always dreamed, & yours for the taking. Truly a lecher's heaven. Yes, everything's perfect, perfect by definition . . . till one afternoon in an unguarded mood you confess to yourself that the cuisine is without flavor & the wine flat, that the celestial muzak piped into your suite, however mellifluous, jangles your nerves. How you wish you could turn on the radio & hear Monk or Dylan or even the six o'clock news. You long, if the truth be known, for a cup of cold water. As for the women, however lovely to look at, to the touch they are as lifeless as the pages of the magazines from which they were drawn & as weightless & predictable as the figments of your own imagination.

It is just then—at that very instant—that the thread of a name & face catches the light on what remains of the delicate film of your cortex, the wraith of a memory . . . & escapes. You call to it desperately over & over, but it will not return, though its residue lingers on your tongue. Such is the other side of God's marvelous amnesia. From that day forward you are lost. You pace in distraction along the Elysian beach obsessed with the need to recall who it was & what it must have been like. How insufferable, at such moments, is the glare of Paradise! & so it is that with only your foolish heart as witness, you begin to long bitterly for home.

The Dumbbell Nebula
(2000)

The Blue Dress

When I grab big Eddie, the gopher drops from his teeth
& bolts for the closet, vanishing
into a clutter of shoes & valises & vacuum attachments
& endless crates of miscellaneous rubbish.
Grumbling & cursing, carton by carton,
I lug everything out
—that mountain of hopeless detritus—until,
with no place to hide, he breaks
for the other side of the room, & I have him at last,
trapped in a corner, tiny & trembling.
I lower the plastic freezer bowl over his head &
                                              Boom!—
slam the thing down.
                        "Got him!" I yell out,
slipping a folder under the edge for a lid.
But when I open the front door it's teeming,
a rain so fierce it drives me back into the house,
& before I can wriggle into my sneakers,
Mary, impatient, has grabbed the contraption
out of my hands & run off into the yard with it, barefoot.
She's wearing that blue house dress.
I know just where she's headed: that big
mossy boulder down by the oleanders
across from the shed,
& I know what she'll do when she gets there—hunker
down, slip off the folder,
let the thing slide to the ground
while she speaks to it softly, whispers
encouraging, comforting things.
Only after the gopher takes a few tentative steps,
dazed, not comprehending how he got back
to his own world, then tries to run off,
will she know how he's fared: if he's wounded,
or stunned, or okay—depraved ravisher

of our gladiolus & roses, but neighbor & kin nonetheless.
Big Eddie meows at my feet while I stand
by the window over the sink, watching
her run back thru the rain,

full of good news: Triumphant. Laughing. Wind
lashing the trees. It's hard to fathom
how gorgeous she looks, running like that
through the storm: that blue
sheath of a dress aglow in the smoky haze—
that luminous blue dress pasted by rain to her hips.
I stand at the window, grinning, amazed
at my own undeserved luck—
at a life that I still, when I think of it, hardly believe.

A Trick

Late afternoon. Huancayo. We'd made the long haul down
from Ayacucho that morning. Were hungry & tired.
Had stumbled into one of those huge, operatic, down-at-the-heels
Peruvian restaurants: red cloths on the tables, teardrop
chandeliers, candles in ribbed silver cages.
Three walls of grey brick, but the wall at the back
the remains of an ancient Quechua temple: that massive,
mortarless, perfectly fitted hand-hewn stone
whose secret had died with the Incas.
Not a soul in the place but a middle-aged waiter
tricked out in the shabby black & white jacket & slacks of the trade.
He brought us two menus, two goblets for wine, a plate
of *papas a la huancaina*. I was unaccountably happy.
In one of those giddy, insouciant moods that come out of nowhere.
The previous summer I'd given the army the slip,
leaving to better men than myself the task of carpet-bombing
the indigent peasants of Asia.
Mary & I had exchanged matrimonial vows in Seattle
& then headed south. Had been bussing for months
from town to town thru the Andes.
The truth is, the whole thing had happened by magic.
                                                    "Hey,
you know that trick where you blow an invisible coin
into a sealed-up glass?" I lowered a saucer over her long-
stemmed goblet so nothing could enter, & grinned
as if I knew how to pluck out of nowhere fishes & loaves.
Mary said No, she didn't—& laughed,
preparing herself for another fine piece of buffoonery.
On the table between us, though it wasn't yet dark,
the candle was already lit. In the distance, the misty sierra.
I asked her to hand me a coin, placed it into my palm,
recited some hocus-pocus known only to shamans from Brooklyn,
then spread out my fingers—& lo & behold, it had vanished!
So far so good. But that part was easy. What I did next

was harder—to blow the invisible coin into that covered-up glass.
The nice thing was you could see it fall in with a clatter,
hear the luxurious clink of silver in glass as it dropped
out of nowhere & settled. Needless to say, she was amazed.
I mean *really* amazed! & so too was our waiter
who, as it turns out, had been watching the whole affair
from the wall by the kitchen, & flew to my side
flailing his arms like a sinner whose soul the Holy
Spirit had entered, & who knows he is saved.
He wanted to know how I'd done it. How such a thing
could possibly happen. *Milagro!* I felt like Jesus
raising the dead: a little embarrassed, but pleased
that I'd brought the thing off—& that someone had seen it.
Huancayo. I liked the looks of the place: that sharp
mountain light before dusk, folks walking around
on the other side of the window in woolen serapes.
& no less amazing, sitting beside me, all forbearance & grace, that angelic young
woman who'd fallen somehow into my life, & more miraculous still, had vowed
she would love me forever. If it wouldn't have sounded so pious
or grandiose, I'd have said to that fellow: "Friend,
how I did it isn't really the point; in this world nothing
is more or less marvelous than anything else."
But I didn't. Instead, I just shrugged, the way
that when Lazarus opened his eyes & shook off the dust
& put on his hat, Jesus himself must have shrugged,
as much as to say it was nothing, a trifle. & that done,
we checked out the menus, & taking our new friend's advice
ordered a huge vegetarian feast—me & Mary, my wife,
that woman who one day—all wit & forbearance
& grace—had fallen, by some sort of miracle, into my life.

Perognathus fallax

When I went to the shed to check for water
damage after the last rains,
I found a tiny gray mouse
dead among the stacks of old cartons,
& lifting out the rags & jars,
found his mate, backed in a corner,
tiny & alive. Beside her—ears
barely visible flecks, tails nothing
but tendrils of gray thread—two nurslings:
one curled asleep by her snout,
the other awake at her nipple;
the three together no larger, I'd guess,
than the height of my thumb.
I took the box into the yard,
where there was more light,
& where the cats weren't lurking,
& lifted out the rest of the detritus—
a shredded pillow, cans of varnish
& spray paint—beneath which I found, woven
out of what must have been pieces of cotton,
chewed cardboard & small twigs,
some sort of ramshackle nest.
With nowhere to hide, she scurried
behind it, a pup still at her dugs,
& looked up at me, into my eyes,
the way one of my cats might
who'd been cornered, or as might
one of my own kind, pleading—
her gaze wholly human, wholly intelligible.
It's uncanny, isn't it, how much alike we all are?
The next morning, when I went to the pump
    house
where I'd set the carton for safety,
I was amazed to see
the stunning filigreed globe
into which she had rewoven that nest,

overnight:
from a small port at its top, her little snout
with those two bright eyes,
peering anxiously into my face.
I just stood there. I could hardly believe
how exquisite that nest was,
& how happy I was to see her.
The crumbs of seed I had dropped in
were gone, & I thought how good it would be
to keep them there, safe from the hawks,
feed them whatever they liked—but
for only a moment—then took out my knife
& sliced a small hole in the cardboard,
an inch or so from the bottom,
thinking to let them come & go as they wished.
& the next time I went back they were gone.
I was sorry to see the thing empty.
Is that stupid of me? *Perognathus
fallax*: the San Diego pocket mouse,
according to my *Audubon Guide
to North American Mammals*—
which was the last week of March,
the whole yard given over to mountain lilac
& sage & alyssum, & out by the wood
fence, that stand of iris,
too tattered, I'd thought, to survive
all those hard rains, but which had.
& under my feet, alive,
but so tiny one hardly noticed,
a hundred species of wild flower:
saffron & white & pink & mauve & blood red.

Mysteries

Tonight, sick with the flu & alone, I drift in confusion & neurasthenia
surrendering to the chaos & mystery of all things,
for tonight it comes to me like a sad but obvious revelation
that we know nothing at all. Despite all our fine theories
we don't have the foggiest notion of why or how anything
in this world exists or what anything means or how anything fits
or what we or anyone else are doing here in the first place.
Tonight the whole business is simply beyond me.
Painfully I sit up in bed & look out the window into the evening.
There is a light on in Marie's apartment. My neighbor Marie,
the redhead, is moving away. She found a cheaper apartment
elsewhere. She is packing up her belongings.
The rest of the street is dark, bereft.
In this world, nothing is ruled out & nothing is certain:
savage carnivorous primates bloated with arrogance floating about
on a tiny island among the trillions of islands out in the darkness.
Did you know that the human brain was larger 40 millennia back?
Does that mean they were smarter? It stands to reason they were
but we simply don't know.
& what of the marriage dance of the scorpion? Do whales breach
from exuberance or for some sort of navigational reason?
What does the ant queen know or do to provoke such undying
devotion? What of the coelacanth & the neopilina—not a fossil trace
for 300 million years, then one day there she is swimming around.
In the mangrove swamps the fruit bats hang from the trees & flutter
their great black wings. How does a turnip sprout from a seed?
Creatures that hatch out of eggs & walk about on the earth
as if of their own volition.
How does a leaf unwind on its stem & turn red in the fall & drop
like a feather onto the snowy fields of the spinning world?
What does the shaman whisper into the ear of the beetle
that the beetle repeats to the rain? Why does the common moth
so love the light she is willing to die? Is it some incurable hunger
for warmth? At least that I can understand. How & why
does the salmon swim thousands of miles back to find the precise

streambed, the very rock under which it was born?
God knows what that urge is to be home in one's bed if only to die.
There have been dogs, abandoned by families moving to other
parts of the country, who have followed thru intricate cities,
over the wildest terrain—exhausted & bloody & limping—
a trail that in no way could be said to exist, to scratch at a door
they had never seen, months, in cases, even years later.
Events such as these cannot be explained. If indeed
we are made of the same stuff as sea kelp & stars,
what that stuff is we haven't any idea.
The very atom eludes us. Is it a myth & the cosmos an infinite
series of Chinese boxes, an onion of unending minusculation?
What would it look like apart from the grid of the language—
cut loose from its names? Is there no solid ground
upon which to plant our molecular flag?
What of the microorganic civilizations living their complex
domestic histories out in the roots of our hair?
Is there life in the stars? Are there creatures like us weeping
in furnished rooms out past the solar winds in the incalculable
dark where everything's spinning away from everything else?
Are we just configurations of energy pulsing in space?
As if that explained this!
Is the universe conscious? Have we lived other lives? Does the spirit
exist? Is it immortal? Do these questions even make sense?
& all this weighs on me like a verdict of exile.
I brush back the curtain an inch. It flutters, as if by some ghostly
hand. Now Marie's light is off & the world is nothing again,
utterly vacant, *sunyata*, the indecipherable void. How awesome
& sad & mysterious everything is tonight. Tell me this,
was the Shroud of Turin really the death shroud of Jesus?
What of those tears that gush from the wounds of particular icons?
Don't tell me they don't. Thousands of people have seen them.
Did Therese Newman really survive on a wafer a day?
& the levitations of Eusapia Pallachino & St. Teresa.
& Salsky who suffered the stigmata in that old Victorian mansion
on Oak Street across from the Panhandle on Good Friday.

With my own eyes I saw them—his palms full of blood.
Where does everything disappear that I loved?
The old friends with whom I would wander about
lost in rhapsodic babble, stoned, in the dark:
Jim Fraser, Guarino, Steve Parker & Mednick & Berke—
squabbling & giggling over the cosmos. That walk-up
on 7th Street overlooking the tenement roofs of Manhattan.
Lovely Elizabeth dead & Ronnie OD'd on a rooftop in Brooklyn
& Jerry killed in the war & the women— those dark,
furtive kisses & sighs; all the mysterious moanings of sex.
Where did I lose the addresses of all those people I knew?
Now even their names are gone: taken, lost, abandoned, vanished
into the blue. Where is the *OED* I won at Brooklyn College
for writing a poem & that poem itself decades gone & the black & gold
Madison High School tennis team captain's jacket I was so proud of?
Where is that beaded headband? The marvelous Indian flute?
That book of luminous magic-marker paintings Eliot did?
& where is Eliot now? & Greg Marquez? & Marvin Torfield?
Where are the folding scissors from Avenida Abancay in Lima?
Where is the antique pocket watch Rosalind Eichenstein gave me?
I loved it so—the painted shepherd playing the flute in the greenest,
most minuscule hills. I bet some junkie on 7th Street took it
but there's no way now to find out. It just disappeared,
& no one & nothing that's lost will ever be back.
How came a cuneiform tablet unearthed by the Susquehanna?
Why was Knossos never rebuilt? What blast flattened the Tunguska
forest in 1908? & those things that fall from the sky— manna
from heaven & toads & huge blocks of ice & alabaster
& odd-shaped gelatinous matter— fafrotskis of every description
& type that at one time or another have fallen out of the sky.
The alleged Venezuelan fafrotski— what is it exactly
& where did it come from? & quarks & quasars & black holes....
The woolly mammoth, one moment peacefully grazing on clover
in sunlight, an instant later quick-frozen into the arctic,
antediluvian north. What inconceivable cataclysm occurred?
How did it happen? What would my own children have looked like?

Why is there always one shoe on the freeway?
Why am I shivering? What am I even doing writing this poem?
Is it all nothing but ego—my name screaming out from the grave?
I look out the window again. How strange, now
the tobacco shop on the corner is lit. A gaunt, mustachioed figure
steps to the doorway & looks up at my window & waves.
It's Fernando Pessoa! I wave back—Fernando! Fernando! I cry out.
But he doesn't see me. He can't. The light snaps off.
The tobacco shop disappears into the blackness, into the past . . .
Who was the ghost in the red cape who told Henry IV he would die?
What of those children raised by wolves and gazelles?
What of spontaneous human combustion—those people
who burst into flame? Is space really curved?
Did the universe have a beginning
or did some sort of primal matter always exist?
Either way it doesn't make sense!
How does the pion come tumbling out of the void & where
does it vanish once it is gone? & we too—we too. Into what & where
do we vanish? For the worms, surely we too are meat on the hoof.
Frankly it scares me, it scares the hell out of me.
The back of my neck is dripping with sweat . . . a man with a fever
located somewhere along the Pacific Coast in the latter half
of the 20th century by the Julian calendar: a conscious,
momentary configuration; a bubble in the stew, a child of the dark.
I am going to stand up now if I can—that's what I'm going to do,
& make my way to the kitchen & find the medicine
Mary told me was there. Perhaps she was right.
Perhaps it will help me to sleep.
Yes, that's what I'll do—I'll sleep & forget.
We know only the first words of the message—if that.
I could weep when I think of how lovely it was
in its silver case, all engraved with some sort of floral design,
the antique watch that Rosalind gave me years ago
on the lower east side of Manhattan
when we were young & in love & had nothing but time—
that watch with its little shepherd playing a flute on a tiny hillside,

[48]

gone now like everything else.
Where in the name of Christ did it disappear to—
that's what I want to know!

Beetles

The famous British biologist J.B.S. Haldane,
when asked by a churchman . . . to state
his conception of God, said:
"He is inordinately fond of beetles."
                                        —Primo Levi

Spotted blister beetles. Sacred scarabs.
Water beetles whirling on the surface of still ponds.
Little polka-dotted ladybugs
favored by the Virgin Mary & beloved of children.
Those angelic fireflies sparkling in the summer evenings.
Carrion beetles sniffing out the dead.
June bugs banging into screens.
Click beetles. Tumblebugs. Opossum beetles.
Whirligigs & long-horned rhino beetles.
Cowpea weevils snuggling into beans.
The diving beetle wintering in mud.
Macrodactylus subspinosus: the rose chafer
feasting upon rose petals, dear to the poet Guido
Gozzano. The reddish-brown *Calathus gregarius.*
Iridescent golden brown-haired beetles.
Beetles living in sea wrack, dry wood, loose
gravel. Clown beetles. Pill beetles. Infinitesimal
beetles nesting in the spore tubes of fungi.
There is no climate in which the beetle does not exist,
no ecological niche the beetle does not inhabit,
no organic matter, living, dead, or decomposed
that has not its enthusiast among the beetles,
of whom, it has been estimated, one and one-half
million species currently exist,
which is to say one mortal creature
out of five's a beetle—little armored tank
who has been rolling through the fields her ball of dung

these past three hundred million years: clumsy
but industrious, powerful yet meek,
the lowly, dutiful, & unassuming beetle—
she of whom, among all earth-born creatures, God is fondest.

I Rendezvous with Jim & Lenny at the Barnes

Pretending, as we entered laughing, that we were billionaire collectors,
we agreed that each of us would buy one masterpiece per gallery,
so bounding there from room to room in grinning bliss
we gobbled up Soutines, Bonnards, Modiglianis.
Lenny snagged Monet's boat studio. Jim seized that mauve
felicity of creamy lovers: *Le Bonheur de vivre.* I chose
that terrifying Van Gogh nude, horrific & farouche,
all poverty & pubic hair & suffering.
Together after all those years—three hebephrenic & disheveled
antiquarian collectors from the Dumbbell Nebula.
The museum-goers gave us a wide berth. The guards
eyed us suspiciously & shifted feet.
At closing time we slipped into our coats & left our acquisitions
where they'd hung, & traipsed out into an icy dusk.
In Philadelphia, on Earth, all afternoon, it had been snowing:
a foamy, plush, untouched meringue of snow,
all lacy-blue beneath the streetlights, blanketing the lawns
& trees & roofs & roads of Lower Merion, flakes huge
as piecrusts floating all about us as we clowned & schmoozed
the way we used to carry on back in Manhattan down on 6th Street
in the old days—nothing now, the three of us, but tiny strokes
of silver-gray & orange & maroon, receding past the middle distance—
rapturous, maniacal—high-stepping thru a blizzard of exquisite light.

Lot's Kinky Daughters

were into everything—dildoes, daisychains, muff
& buggery parties, team sex, buff clubs—you name it.
Like everyone else in that scatterbrained town
they were out for a good time
till Yahweh, disgusted, burnt Sodom out of the hills
like a tick, thinking to teach them all a valuable lesson.
That whole voluptuous city in flames
& Lot's wife, bouncing about in the back of the pickup,
wedged in between the jacuzzi & sofa,
suddenly remembers Poopsie the cat
& looks back &— Well, you know the rest.
That night in a cave in the hills above Zoar,
Lot is sprawled out on that couch in a tizzy,
his simpleton daughters down at his feet in their pj's
trying to figure it out. "Well, it's mean if you ask me,"
the older one pouts. "Mama was nice,
& this place is creepy & boring."
"It must have been some kind of lesson," the younger one
adds. "But about what?" & she yawns from the effort,
then reaching under the pillow pulls out the blackberry
schnapps that she managed to salvage.
Two shots & they're lit like a bordello switchboard on payday,
the three of them cackling & panting & ripe to kindle
the tribes of Ben Ami & Moab—their shadows
in candlelight folding together & swirling about like some
sort of angel—but darker, with translucent limbs,
& misshapen wings, & immense genitalia.

Romero

By early December the dirt road will be nicely macadamed,
& the backcountry dust will no longer blow through the window
into my hair. In the chill of the oncoming winter
I'll rise from my chair & throw pitch-pine & oak on the fire—look,
it is nearly winter already! By now Romero
should either be up around Fresno, working construction,
or back in Tuxtla Gutierrez, yoked to a cart of *paletas*,
& mending his socks—& plotting another go at the States.
When he stepped from the canyon I pulled to the shoulder
& opened the door. We were north of Tecate: the border patrol
swarming over the highway. Did I have any neighbor,
he wanted to know, who needed a worker?
So all morning, at my place, we cut back the wild chamise
by the shed, though we ended up arguing over money:
he wouldn't take a cent—that was to pay me for picking him up
in the first place. "Romero, for god's sakes
you can't work for nothing!"—& kept at him until he relented.
Mary, what fine enchiladas! what heavenly pears!
How exhausted he was, & dusty & hungry & hopeful!
Late in the evening, we wove our way out of the mountains:
the Barrett grade thru Dulzura down to Spring Valley
& north to Santee. It was August. The night sky a bucket
of coins spilling over the hills. Now & then meteors
flared thru the darkness & vanished. "Right here
is good," he said on a back street, at a grove of black
eucalyptus. I pulled to the curb. It was where he would sleep.
In the morning, a truck cruising Magnolia
would take him to Fresno,
where *la migra* was scarce & plenty of guys like himself,
without papers, were working construction. He slung his blanket
over his shoulder, picked up his bag, & asked me again
in his broken, measured, tentative English, please
to thank my *Maria bonita* for all of her kindness. I said that I would.
"Romero, take care. . . ." & under those fugitive stars

we gave each other a long, final *abrazo*. Country
of endless abundance & workers with nowhere to sleep.
"Esteban, I. . . ." —& he nodded, & turned,
& walked off into that tunnel of trees & was gone.

Refugees, Late Summer Night

Woke with a start, the dogs barking out by the fence,
yard flooded with light. Groped my way to the window.
Out on the road a dozen quick figures
hugging the shadows: bundles slung at their shoulders
& water jugs at their hips. You could hear,
under the rattle of wind, as they passed,
the crunch of sneakers on gravel. *Pollos.* Illegals
who'd managed to slip past the Border Patrol,
its Broncos & choppers endlessly circling
the canyons & hills between here & Tecate.
Out there, in the dark, they could have been
anyone: refugees from Rwanda, slaves pushing north.
Palestinians, Gypsies, Armenians, Jews . . . .
The lights of Tijuana, that yellow haze to the west,
could have been Melos, Cracow, Quang Ngai . . . .
I watched from the window till they were lost
in the shadows. Our motion light turned itself off.
The dogs gave a last, perfunctory bark
& loped back to the house: those dry, rocky hills
& the wild sage at the edge of the canyon
vanishing too. Then stared out at nothing.
No sound anymore but my own breath,
& the papery click of the wind in the leaves
of that parched eucalyptus: a rattle of bones;
chimes in a doorway; history riffling its pages.

Ronnie

Shortly after they'd scrambled his brain with electroshock,
I bumped into him on a Brooklyn street.
He had put on some weight, seemed calmer, less jangled.
No longer the manic young poet who'd bounce
about on the balls of his feet, barely touching
the street as he floated above it—
he had tricked back that garland of black curls,
sported, of all things, a jacket & tie,
& seemed, for once, at home in his body—grounded
the way the rest of us are, by the world's weight.
        "Steve, I feel great!"
though his voice, too quick & emphatic,
made me uneasy: "A million times better off!"
And he opened his fist in a little explosion of fingers & thumb,
by way of dismissing, as if it hadn't really been his,
that earlier life:
        "Though sometimes . . . I . . .
I guess I forget things . . . ." & with that
it collapsed: the sanguine, implacable mask electro-
convulsive shock had made of his face
crumbled along the line of his mouth, & his eyes went hazy.
He looked scared, like a man who wakes up
& doesn't know where he is, his own name, what city
he's in, or whose body: that old,
impetuous storm squelched to a kind of stolid confusion.
        The northeast heaves,
            O loveliest of winds to me—
a line from one of his exquisite Hölderlin versions
swam through my head. The street glistened with rain.
Leaves spun at our feet. We made the sort of talk
people make. Shook hands: "Ronnie,
it's great to see you again!" Only an awkward civility
kept me from hugging him, weeping—& then hurried off,
though thirty years later, having heard he was gone,

I set the phone to its cradle & stood
in the dark, wrenched back to that street
& to all that had never got said, & that telling you of
has taken me back to again—the sorrow
& love I had left there, unspoken between us:
his fitful, disquieted spirit; the poem of his life whirling
about in my head—a tumult of leaves in a gust of uneasy wind.

Solo Monk

One day back in the '60s
Monk was sitting at the piano,
Charlie Mingus pulling at his coat
how Monk should put the word in
so the Mingus group
could play The Five Spot,
seeing as how Monk's already legendary gig
down there was ending—
        Mingus,
all persuasion & cajolery,
ran it down for twenty minutes
till he capped it with the comment:
    "Dig it, Thelonious,
        you know we Black Brothers
    GOT to stick together!"
At which point, Monk,
laconic to a fault
(till then he hadn't said a word), turned
slowly with a sidewise glance
& raised one eyebrow:
        "Ma-aan,"
    he said,
"I thought you was Chi-nese!"

       & evenings, between sets,
Monk would pace outside The Five Spot,
head cocked to some inner keyboard.
With that listing gait of his,
that wispy black goatee,
that rumpled herringbone tweed hat
he sported in those days,
he'd pace that corner, solitary
       & quixotic
    in a rapture

of exploding chords—
        all angular
     & dissonant
            & oddly phrased.

One summer night a Checker Cab
pulled up as he was so engaged,
            & Monk,
who happened to be passing at that moment,
swung back the door,
then stepped so quietly
& self-effacingly behind it
that you would have thought it was his calling—
but his ear as ever cocked
        to that imaginary keyboard.

                       An elegant patrician couple, clubbing,
—blond Westchester money—
stepped out on 8th Street like an ad for Chivas Regal.
        As the primped fox
sashayed past him in her saffron strapless,
tossing back her golden mane,
her escort nodded vaguely
not so much as glancing up
at that solicitous, albeit altogether funky
looking colored doorman
           with the goofy hat:
A gesture almost too indifferent to be haughty.
& with that they hurried past & disappeared
into The Five Spot,
having come to hear the legendary Monk,
that droll & idiosyncratic piano.
    The sensation, Whitney Balliett wrote,
    of missing the bottom step in the dark.

"—Eerie, isn't it,
to hear him playing
tho he's dead,"
Mary said, playing Monk
the night we heard
he had died.
& she lowered the dust cover
over the turntable
as quietly as Monk had shut the door
of that Checker Cab
& turning without sign or gesture
had gone off
bopping down the street,
head cocked as ever to one side
& circled by the halo
of that rumpled hat:
oblivious . . .
preoccupied . . .
lost
in the sweet jazz of the night—
Monk
on 8th Street
at the end of summer
in the early '60s.
Must have been around 11:55.

I Attend a Poetry Reading

The fellow reading poetry at us wouldn't stop.
Nothing would dissuade him:
not the stifling heat; the smoky walls
with their illuminated clocks;
our host, who shifted anxiously
from foot to foot.
Polite applause had stiffened
to an icy silence:
no one clapped
or nodded.
No one sighed.
Surely he must understand that we had families
waiting for us, jobs
we had to get to in the morning.
That chair was murdering my back.
The cappuccino
tasted unaccountably of uric acid.
Lurid bullfight posters flickered
in the red fluorescent light—
& suddenly I knew that I had died,
& for those much too windy readings of my own
had been condemned
to sit forever in this damned café.
A squadron of enormous flies
buzzed around the cup of piss
I had been drinking from.
Up at the mike, our poet of the evening
grinned,
& flicked his tail,
& kept on reading.

Metaphysics

The trouble with me is I have a low metaphysical threshold.
When I'm told the bicameral mind can never know things in themselves,
I shake my head gravely . . . but simply out of politeness.
Frankly, the conflict between the noumenal & phenomenal worlds
means nothing to me whatsoever.
Is perceptual knowledge constrained by the categorical space
in which language unfolds,
or is Absolute Is-ness provoked by the Relative Ought?
"Well, I'd never quite thought of things in that light . . . "
I stammer & cough. I help myself to the cheese dip.
Perhaps I'm obtuse, but I could never recall whether it's Essence
that precedes Existence, or the other way round. The fact is
I'd rather my pinky get slammed in the door of a semi than argue
over the epistemological underpinnings of post-deconstruction,
whether signifiers are self-referential, or meaning culture-specific.
It's knotty alright, I say, stifling a yawn.
The question of course is who is that redhead,
the one at the other end of the room with the lavender
lipstick & radical décolletage? & why
at these awful soirées do I always get stuck among the professors?
If it isn't free-will, they are beating to death the mind-body dilemma,
the transcendental nature of Time, that gut-wrenching issue:
does or does not the external world really exist?
Ah, now she is crossing her legs!
I help myself to the pretzels. I pour some more wine.
Let them build the City of God out of earwax & toothpicks without me.
And what, pray tell, is the meaning of Meaning?
Are Existence & Nothingness one & the same?
And how in the Bright Night of Dread does the body of ontic Being arise?
I shake my head, as much as to say I too am perplexed.
Politeness itself, I am loath to point out that perhaps what we need
is more daylight & less metaphysics.
As if this world isn't perfectly real as it is, or as real as it gets,
they want us to think that the world behind it is better,

that the dead are elsewhere & happy,
that our loved ones are waiting for us on the other side of *samsara*.
As if that sort of cerebral monoxide could stifle
the groans of the dying, the winds of disaster, the weeping
that's left here behind us. & still they go on.
Armageddon itself would not be enough to dissuade them!
Is Spirit immortal? Do dreams occupy space? Is the universe
purposeful, random, unbounded, autogenous, finite, alive?
Is death an illusion? Or simply another sort of beginning?
A journey indeed—but whither & whence?
Yes, yes! I say, my head spinning.
It's utterly fascinating! Who would have guessed it!
Far off in the night, a coyote howls at the moon.
I have by now finished the cheese dip, the pretzels, the wine.
The lickerish redhead has long since slipped off
on the arm of her lover—some young, good-looking swine.
I rise with a hundred regrets, thanking my hosts,
zipping my jacket, & spouting farewells in every direction:
It's certainly something to ponder, I tell them,
but really, I have to get going.
It's late & tomorrow I'm up bright & early.
A marvelous evening! Your quiche by the way was divine!

Dusk in the Cuyamacas

It was that tangerine
& golden
sepia light
spilling over the Cuyamacas
—each leaf
of the manzanita
chiseled in space—
that shook me out of my dreams
till I woke again
to my own life:
everything shimmering,
everything just as it is.

The Workout

Decked out in purple shorts & spandex tights & party-colored jogging suits,
the votaries of fitness have been trying to shape up.
While dervishes of Monday evening high-impact aerobics
leap & jerk like frenzied zealots in convulsive seizure,
& those dumbbell lifters grunting into full-length mirrors
spend their workouts flirting with themselves,
with their own sweet pumped-up repetitions,
other flagellants have strapped their limbs to squat-&-flex devices,
chest expanders, hip & thigh racks, & are climbing dutifully the gravitronic
exer-stairway up toward skinny heaven.
Not unlike the penitents of other sects, they are convinced that decades
of decay can be undone, & that the more one genuflects
the less one rots — a doctrine that has got the aged, the adipose
& the misshapen pedaling their stationary bikes in such unholy fury
you would think they were outracing Time, that hag who has been waiting
at the finish line to snip the thread, & will not be outrun.
While every now & then some sleek young thing in leotards
parades her killer body to remind the women what they do not look like,
& the men what they are not about to have the pleasures of,
however long they bicycle in place.
A carnival of dreams is all it is, this imbecilic adoration of the golden calf
& bulging chest & tapered thigh, this robegalia of compulsive nitwits
& deluded fools, is just what I am thinking, when I spot him riding toward me
in that mirror, flushed & puffing: my unpleasant-looking older cousin
with that stupid grin— as smug & supercilious as ever: haggard,
baggy-eyed & self-impressed, his drooping middle thicker
than I'd ever have supposed. Humiliated, frankly, to be seen with him,
especially in such a place as this, I turn my gaze discreetly elsewhere,
for God knows we never have had all that much in common—I being
by a long shot younger, more athletic, slender, muscular & better looking.

Notice

This evening, the sturdy Levis
I wore every day for over a year
& which seemed to the end
in perfect condition,
suddenly tore.
How or why I don't know,
but there it was: a big rip at the crotch.
A month ago my friend Nick
walked off a racquetball court,
showered,
got into his street clothes,
& halfway home collapsed & died.
Take heed, you who read this,
& drop to your knees now & again
like the poet Christopher Smart
& kiss the earth & be joyful
& make much of your time
& be kindly to everyone,
even to those who do not deserve it.
For although you may not believe
it will happen,
you too will one day be gone.
I, whose Levis ripped at the crotch
for no reason,
assure you that such is the case.
Pass it on.

Basic

The first thing that they do is shave your head
& scream into your face until you drop
the pleasant fiction that had been your life.
More quickly than you would have guessed
you learn obedience: to shut your mouth
& do what you are told; that you survive
by virtue of compliance, shutting down.
When they scream "drop for twenty," then you drop.
If wobbly from lack of sleep,
you're told to sit up half the night & strip
your M-1 down, that's what you do. You strip it down.
The only insubordination's in your eyes, that can't
accept the order not to close. Your combat boots
kept so compulsively spit-shined
you see your face in both hard toes—skinned
to the scalp, pathetically distorted,
not unrecognizable but not quite you—a self
that marches dutifully through sleet & has perfected
the low crawl.
    One gray morning in the second week
of basic training, lacing up his boots,
that shy, phlegmatic, red-haired boy who bunked
above me whispered,
                "Steve,
I don't believe I'm gonna make it . . . ."
"No way, man! You're doing fine! Hey look, c'mon, we're late,"
& shrugged him off to race out just in time
to make formation in the mist
of that Kentucky morning.
—He was right. He didn't. He took a razor blade that night,
& crawling underneath the barracks slashed his throat.
What little of myself I saved in there
I saved by microscopic gestures of defiance:
Instead of screaming *Kill*, I'd plunge my bayonet

into that dummy screaming *Quill* . . . . *Nil* . . .
At rifle drill I'd hum the *Internationale*
& fire fifty feet above the target. I kept Dexedrines
in my fatigues. Took heart from the seditious drollery
of Sergeant May, that L.A. homeboy
with the black goatee, all hip panache & grace:
that bop salute and smart-ass version of left face.
& sometimes from his cadre room at night, the wailing
blues of Ray Charles drifted through the barracks,
& I'd lie there in the dark, awake—remembering
that other life that I had left behind.
& it was Sergeant May & Ray Charles
& Dexedrine that got me through.
Had I been more courageous, less the terrified recruit
who did what he was told, I would have hung back
with that boy & argued with him,
said whatever needed saying
or at least have heard him out, just listened, or let
someone know . . . or somehow, god knows, saved him.
But I wasn't. & I didn't.
I was just a kid myself.
For all my revolutionary rhetoric, I shut my eyes
& ears, when shutting of the eyes & ears was politic.
When they said strip your M-1 down, I stripped it down.
When they said march, I marched.

Alpha Centauri

We were down at the Hungry Hunter's
after a peace march, when Danny,
whose passions are social justice
& roast cornish hen,
starts whipping himself into a frenzy
over the President's lies,
multinational greed,
the Pentagon's genocidal agenda.
"The exploitation of anyone,"
Danny says, lifting that small bird's body
in both of his hands
& tearing a wing off,
"oppresses us all!"
& with that he starts in on the rape of the Congo,
slavery in Cape Town,
torture in Turkey,
El Salvador,
Poland,
Afghanistan,
Alpha Centauri . . .
Ripping the last bit of flesh with his teeth,
Danny says there are millions of corpses
under our noses
that nobody sees.
& when everyone else at the table agrees,
he shakes his head as much as to say
it's beyond comprehension,
& wipes a trickle of grease from his chin,
crumbling his napkin onto a plate
full of bones & pieces of skin & left-over peas.

Last Will

If I am ever unlucky enough to die (God forbid!)
I would like to be propped up in my orange overstuffed chair
with my legs crossed, dressed in my favorite sweater & jeans
& embalmed in a permanent glaze like a donut, or Lenin,
a small bronze plaque on the door of my study
showing the dates of my incarnation & death.
& leave the room as it was! Let nothing be touched in the house!
My underpants stuck on the doorknob just where I left them.
My dental floss lying on top of the *Bhagavad Gita* next to my socks.
Let the whole of Ebers Street be roped off & planted with yew trees
from Narragansett to Cape May & left as a monument to my passing.
The street? No—the city itself! Henceforth let it be known
as the Steve M. Kowit Memorial Park & Museum.
Better yet, if the thing can be done without too much fuss
put the whole planet to sleep. Let the pigeons & buses
& lawyers & ladies hanging out wash freeze in their tracks.
Let the whole thing be preserved under ice just as it looked
when the last bit of drool trickled over my chin.
Let the last of the galaxies sizzle out like a match in the wind
& the cosmic balloon shrink down to a noodle & screech to a halt.
Let time clot like a pinprick of blood & the great solar flame
flicker down to the size of a *yertzite* candle leaving the universe dark
but for one tiny spotlight trained on the figure of me propped in my chair—
for after my death what possible reason could life in any form
care to exist? —Don't you see it would be utterly pointless!
I would be gone! Look, try to conceive it, a world without *me*! Me
entirely absent—nobody here with these eyes, this name, these teeth!
Nothing but vacant space; a dry sucking wind where I walked,
where I sat— where you used to see me you would see
nothing at all! I tell you it dwarfs the imagination!
Oh yes, one last thing: the right leg is to be crossed over the left
— I prefer it that way — & poised on the knee. Prop
the left elbow up on the arm of the chair with a pen in my right hand—
let my left be characteristically scratching my skull or pulling my hair.
If you wish close the lids of my eyes but whatever you do
the mouth must remain open just as it was in life—
yes, open forever! On that I absolutely insist!

[71]

Hell

I died & went to Hell & it was nothing like L.A.
The air all shimmering & blue. No windows
busted, gutted walk-ups, muggings, rapes.
No drooling hoodlums hulking in the doorways.
Hell isn't anything like Ethiopia or Bangladesh or Bogota:
Beggars are unheard of. No one's starving. Nobody
lies moaning in the streets. Nor is it Dachau
with its ovens, Troy in flames, some slaughterhouse
where screaming animals, hung upside down, are bled & skinned.
No plague-infested Avignon or post-annihilation Hiroshima.
Quite the contrary: in Hell everybody's health is fine
forever, & the weather is superb—eternal spring.
The countryside all wildflowers & the cities
hum with commerce: cargo ships bring all the latest
in appliances, home entertainment, foreign culture, silks.
Folks fall in love, have children. There is sex
& romance for the asking. In a word, the place is perfect.
Only, unlike heaven, where when it rains
the people are content to let it rain,
in Hell they live like we do—endlessly complaining.
Nothing as it is is ever right. The astroturf
a nuisance, neighbors' kids too noisy, traffic
nothing but a headache. If the patio were just
a little larger, or the sunroof on the Winnebago worked.
If only we had darker eyes or softer skin or longer legs,
lived elsewhere, plied a different trade, were slender,
sexy, wealthy, younger, famous, loved, athletic.
Friend, I swear to you as one who has returned
if only to bear witness: no satanic furies
beat their kited wings. No bats shriek overhead.
There are no flames. No vats of boiling oil
wait to greet us in that doleful kingdom.
Nothing of the sort. The gentleman who'll ferry you across
is all solicitude & courtesy. The river black but calm.
The crossing less eventful than one might have guessed.
Though no doubt you will think it's far too windy on the water.

That the glare is awful. That you're tired, hungry, ill
at ease, or that, if nothing else, the quiet is unnerving,
that you need a drink, a cigarette, a cup of coffee.

Jacumba

I am sitting in the restaurant of the spiffy
new air-conditioned Jacumba Motel
& Health Spa, sipping a root beer
& staring out at a desert
so blazingly desiccated & stark
it's hard to imagine that anything
other than lizards & buckthorn survives here,
& wondering where the old Jacumba Hotel
disappeared to,
that rambling, stucco monstrosity
where one summer night we. . . .
Well, what's the use. Without that hotel
this town is nothing at all of the crumbling,
moth-infested ghost-town it was,
blistering out in the Anza Borrego,
halfway to Yuma,
exquisitely shabby & brooding.
Ah, Time—with your ferocious improvements!
Your infernal, confounded meddling!

Some Clouds

Now that I've unplugged the phone
no one can reach me—
At least for this one afternoon
they will have to get by without my advice or opinion.
Now nobody else is going to call
& ask in a tentative voice
if I haven't yet heard that she's dead,
that woman I once loved—
nothing but ashes scattered over a city
that barely itself any longer exists.
Yes, thank you, I've heard.
It had been too lovely a morning.
That in itself should have warned me.
The sun lit up the tangerines
& the blazing poinsettias
like so many candles.
For one afternoon they will have to forgive me.
I am busy watching things happen again
that happened a long time ago,
as I lean back in Josephine's lawn chair
under a sky of incredible blue,
broken—if that is the word for it—
by a few billowing clouds,
all white & unspeakably lovely,
drifting out of one nothingness into another.

Kiss

On the patio of that little cafe in the Del Mar Plaza
across from the Esmeralda Bookstore, where you can
sit sipping latté & look out past the Pacific
Coast Highway onto the ocean, a couple is tangled
in one of those steamy, smoldering kisses.
His right arm coils her waist, arching her back
& drawing her toward him. He could be Sicilian,
or Lebanese, with that gorgeous complexion,
those chiseled forearms, that clutch of dark curls.
The young woman's skirt, lilac & sheer, lifts
as she stretches, levitated out of her sandals, out
of her body, her head flung back, fingers
wrapped in his curls. Her long chestnut hair
spills toward her thighs as she clings to his mouth,
to his loins, to his chest. How wickedly
beautiful both of them are! To their left,
off the North County coast, on an infinite sea,
two sailboats triangulate heaven. In the sheen
of the morning, you munch an apricot scone
& sip your cafe latté, that blue cup of light at your lips,
with its genie of steam. In its vase, on your table,
a white tea rose shimmers. Your fork
shines on its plate. Everything trembles & glows.

The First Noble Truth

(2007)

To Tell the Literal Truth

is the trick by which poetry, Rico was saying, anchors itself
to the actual world (I had been rash enough to suggest
that in art the literal truth doesn't matter a bit),
when an uncoiling rattler, a good four feet of her stretched
in the heat on the ill-marked Moorfred Rivercrest
trail we'd been hiking, startled us out of our chatter.
We didn't breathe, gave her a wide berth, & were safely past,
when Zoly, our Aussie companion, who'd just gotten back
from a month-long dig in the outback pits of Rodinga
—Zoly, who cares not a whit for epistemological theory—
did something I'll never forget: in one swift motion swiveled,
bent & grabbed for her throat, the other hand closing
above that whiplash of rattles, then, with a grin, rose to his feet.
The creature writhed in his hands, buzzed with her hideous
rattlers, while she hissed with her godawful tongues
& tried to break free. Rico & me, we jumped back in terror.
Zoly, holding her out for us to admire, said "*Crotalus atrox:*
Western Diamondback. Marvelous specimen, no?"
I could care less what it was called. I took another step back.
Zoly strode to an outcrop of boulders a few yards away,
& gently as setting a kid in its crib, & with only the tiniest
flourish—the sort a jaunty conductor or close-up
magician might make—tossed the thing free.
It vanished, instantaneously, slithering into the rocks.
I took a deep breath & relaxed. From where we stood,
on that rise, you could make out the Salton Sea far
to the east, & the undulant floor of the desert a long drop below,
endless & dreamlike. "Amazing!" Rico mumbled
under his breath, lifting his Padres cap & rubbing the sweat
from his brow. But whether he meant the vista, or snake,
or how quickly it vanished, or what Zoly had done,
or the whole delectable drift of the thing, god only knows.
Listen: In art, the truth—in that sense—doesn't matter.
I made the whole story up. The Aussie. The outback.

The snake. Even the name of the trail. All but the part
where two friends & I argue over the poet's
relationship to the literal fact. Everything else in this poem is a lie.

for Al Zolynas & Fred Moramarco

Will Boland & I

stroll from Dog Beach down to Cape May, grumbling
over this nation's inexhaustible predilection for carnage:
the mask of rectitude painted over the skull of vindictive rage.
It is midwinter, the beach all but deserted:
an elderly gent walks an elderly golden retriever;
a family of four is out hunting for shells;
two good old boys chugging their Michelobs
take in the last of the sunset: down at their feet,
Iwo Jimaed into the sand, a colossal American flag
that they've lugged down here to the beach
with their cooler of beer to cheer on the home team.
Night & day, on the other side of the world,
daisy-cutters are pounding a village to shambles, bathing
the landscape in blood.
Women crouch in the rubble rocking their dead.
                    —*Listen*, I say to Will.
E. O. Wilson can swear up & down there are species
of ants even more compulsively fratricidal than man:
I, for one, remain unconvinced.

Above us, that gorgeous midwinter dusk:
at our feet, the Pacific, ablaze in magentas & red.
True enough, he ventures, *but Steve, you've got to admit*
we're just as much a part of this world as anything else . . .
& maybe, in some crazy way, marvelous too!
                         I shrug.
We walk on in silence.
A couple of high-school girls,
frolicking in & out of the surf, smile up at us sweetly.
          A part of this world yes, I snarl back.
But surely the ugliest part!—the words hardly out of my mouth
when those two young women, now twenty yards or so
down the beach, suddenly fling open their arms, rise to their toes,
leap into the air, & float there—angelic . . . unearthly . . .
impossibly luminous creatures, alighting at last in a dazzle
of pirouettes & glissades, only to rise up into the air again & again,

while Will & I stand there—dumbfounded, grinning, amazed.
under the flare of the night's first stars
each *grande jeté* more splendid, rapturous, vaulting!
Two ardently schooled young ballerinas,

silhouetted against the indigo flames
of the darkening western horizon.
The last of the light of this world setting behind them.

The First Noble Truth

They loved *Siddhartha*. No surprises there! But when I pick up
the chalk & scratch on the board *DUKKA: The First
Noble Truth—Suffering permeates life*, no one looks pleased.
After a moment of general grumbling Marie Elena
mumbles aloud *I'm not sure that's true*. Then Deegan
pipes in *Buddha Deluda*—& that breaks the ice & everyone
laughs. But a laugh with an edge, a laugh that buzzes
around the room the way damaged wires back in the walls
sizzle before they're ready to blow. Then Carlos Padilla leaps
to his feet & says *Suffering—No way! That's just the crud
you wipe from your hands,* mendrugos *you shake from your hair!
This life is joy to the max! Just padding around in bare feet,
or sipping an icy Fanta, or sprawling out on the grass doing
lunch with a couple of homies.* . . . Feisty, full of exuberant health
& good looks & high spirits, Carlos defending our common lot
with such good-natured, passionate faith even I can't help
but grin, cheering him on. When he's done with that funny harangue,
almost everyone laughs; half a dozen start clapping. But others
remain unconvinced: It's there on their faces. Some of the older
ones in the back of the room, & Sean & Ty—& Ahmad for sure.
While the ones filled with the pleased, undauntable juices of life
are clapping & laughing, these others smile uneasily,
discomforted, silent . . . Bradley stares at the back of his hand.
Grace Huerta listens politely, stroking her long, gray beautiful hair.
To my left, the clock on the wall is much too insistently ticking away.
Time to stop all this chatter, time to release the slew of us back
into this piercingly rapturous, inexplicably marvelous world—world
that is everywhere freighted with sorrow: *Dukka*: the First Noble Truth.

The Burro

That little plaster donkey we had bought while waiting
at the San Ysidro-Tijuana border crossing years ago
was—but for the burnt umber they had painted her—
a perfect likeness of those burros climbing thru the mist-bound
mountains of Chiapas, bundles of firewood lashed
to their backs & their slender necks bowed slightly
in the harness: unhappy servants of the people
who had built Copan, carved Palenque, plotted the ecliptic
for a thousand years before the pious Spanish Christians
came to swing them from the trees & steal their land. At dawn,
each week, indians from Tenejapa & San Juan Chamula
would trot out of the hills, pack animals themselves,
hunched under bundles of *leña* & *carbon*.
One family or another would tap timorously at the door
of our adobe house in San Cristobal, & I'd open it & nod:
Si, bueno, yes, of course! & grateful & relieved they'd ease
the tumplines from their brows & slide those heavy
bundles from their backs & then unload the patient, small, dust-
colored burro who'd be standing by them in the courtyard,
dutiful & somber & resigned. Half the night they had been
climbing down those rocky mountain footpaths through the dark.
Not just grown men but women & young kids, many of them
barefoot, buffered from the cold in nothing but those threadbare
black *chamarras*, & we would pay for all that wood & charcoal
with a few measly pesos & a handful of tortillas.
With a crack, like the lash of a whip, that little souvenir
shop burro shattered one spring morning of her own weight,
shards of chalky plaster scattering beneath the picture
window where she'd stood, who silently, for years, had been
a keepsake to us of that other life—long-suffering servant
of the servants of the Mexican sierra: that little plaster burro
at the window in the light, by the blue ceramic bell from Tuxtla,
& the black Oaxacan flute, & the African violets, & the wandering Jew.

Snapshot

At night, a man is sitting at his desk in pain, aging,
full of fears & dreams, till Jesse barges in
& nuzzles his left leg & says, *Hey,*
you know that open box of milk bones
in the kitchen? Well, I've been thinking . . .
The man washes down another Vicodin,
scratches the dog's head, & the two of them
get up & leave the room. When he returns,
he sees how dark it is outside, & late.
He types & stops, looking for a phrase he can't
quite find, some gesture that the past
had given him & taken back.
Above his desk, that ancient snapshot of his folks,
two Lower East Side kids, their lives together
just beginning, who will never understand
that everything the future holds for them
has passed. Dexter Gordon's hushed
& melancholic take on "Don't Explain" drifts
quietly across the room, as if that saxophone
knew, somehow, that the fellow staring
at that photo had been weeping, stupidly
& over nothing. At the keyboard, Sonny Clark
looks over once at Dex & nods, & shuts
his eyes, & listens to himself—to both of them.
Staring out the window at the dark,
the man finds, he thinks, at last,
what he's been looking for, & goes on typing.

After Surgery

I hobble up the driveway holding Mary's arm & leaning
on that old collapsible black cane
that years ago I thought I'd put away for good.
A week ago this life was nothing but intolerable pain,
but now it's rather wonderful again.
Raymond, goofily delighted that we're strolling
thru the dark, lopes on ahead: *Make way! Make way!*
he barks excitedly. An all but moonless night
in which we have stepped out to look at Mars,
just past the driveway, over the Tecate hills, huge
& glowing in the eastern sky & closer to the Earth
than it has been in slightly under sixty thousand years.
—*No,* Mary shakes her head, *that can't be Mars.*
That thing's too bright . . . too big. Peering at it
through those old binoculars, she tells me that she's certain
what it is I've been admiring up there is just another
border patrol chopper hovering above the canyons
between here & Mexico, chasing down some band
of hapless *campesinos* working their way north.
—*No, It's Mars alright! I'd recognize it anywhere!*
I say authoritatively, as is my wont.
& pointing with that hollow cane of mine
to where it gleams—as bold & asymmetrical
as any of those feverish looking asterisks I scribble
in the margins of my books, marking passages
that seem absolutely right or marvelously put, & worth
(O sweet & foolish dream) returning to someday
when I have time—I patiently explain to her that Mars
is just where it's supposed to be: straight up
the driveway, past Coyote Holler Road, where we ourselves
are standing, looking east. Gleeful, tail awag,
Ray hunkers down & looks east too, expectantly,
while I, inspired at last, & flourishing that hollow wand of mine,
as Johannes Kepler might himself have, centuries ago,
trace, among that intricate vast circuitry of stars,
the constellation of Krokidium (the bloated frog),

& Balthor & Valdubius—exactly where they'd have
no choice but find themselves this time of night
above the planet Earth, there in the August sky.
Mary, dutifully impressed, takes my arm
& heads us back, suggesting that for all we know
there's not a single one of all these stars that even
has existed for a million years. *Ridiculous!* I bellow.
*If they didn't exist just how the hell could we be looking
up at them?!* To which she mumbles something
that I won't repeat, & kisses me, & slips her arm
around my waist & says it's nice to have me home.
I wince, & hobble eight or ten more feet, & look up
at the sky for one last time, & tell her just what any
self-respecting star might well have said if it could speak:
Honey, you can't believe how glad I am I still exist.

Translator's Note

Friend, if these verses
seem inconsequential
& clumsy,
a macaronic concoction
of tortured devices,
metrical gaffes,
& bloated conceits,
incapable
for so much as a single
figure or phrase
of wrenching the spirit
awake
to the rapture
& grief of this world,
please keep in mind
that what you've been reading
are nothing
but quickly assembled
slipshod translations.
O patient,
long-suffering reader,
I swear it
upon all I hold sacred:
In the original tongue
these poems
are absolutely sublime.

Rest Stop

To piss, I pull into the rest stop off Interstate 10, halfway
between Tucson & Casa Grande. It's three in the morning,
the scented sage desert so delectably hot
I could weep. Then too, there's that full orange moon,
almost too big to be true. Man's fate, when all's said & done,
isn't the issue. On the wall above the urinal someone
has scrawled LIBERATE JESUS. Huh? Liberate Jesus?
Outside, a fellow who's fallen asleep in the bed of his pickup
is happily snoring. Three young dudes hunker
by the stone fountain smoking & shooting the bull.
An elderly woman leans on her walker,
sucking the juice from a pear. Behind
her, a handful of unlit rec-v's. Then nothing but desert:
palo verdes & yucca. Not a single subdivision or mall.
After we're gone—not just this infinitely sanctimonious
nation-state, but the whole duplicitous, bloodthirsty
human tribe—it will still be here. Well pleased, I slide
back into my little yellow Tercel & cruise onto 10 West.
The woman with her walker, the guy catching some Zs,
the buddies hunkering there in the night, smoking
& chatting, I wish them all well. I slip in another CD:
Hollow Bamboo. Figure to make Yuma by dawn.
I think of that God of Love flinging millions of souls
into Hell, of the puffed-up, fantastic beliefs
of this tiny featherless biped. That aside,
the night about as fragrant & paradisiacal as it gets.
Spectacular moon low in the west. Ry Cooder's
guitar. Ronu Majumdar's bamboo flute. Desert on both sides.

A Betrayal

A friend I hadn't seen in more than three decades wrote
to tell me he had just remarried, and was finally happy.
This followed by a long denunciation of his former wife,
whom I had known back then when all of us were young,
& who, through tireless manipulation & deceit (or
so he claimed) had won full custody of the kids, ruining
two decades of his life. "She would not even show me
the room where the children slept," he wrote, "or so much
as offer me a cup of water from the kitchen tap."
I was shocked, though at the same time couldn't help
but think of that afternoon a few weeks after their first son
had been born, when he'd dropped by, exuberantly happy,
& in the midst of laughing about how little sleep they
were getting, mentioned, in passing, that they had taken Pica,
their lovable Irish setter, back to the pound: "With an infant
in the house . . .," he started to explain, the way one might
about a troublesome TV or a sofa bed returned for taking
too much space up in the den. My mouth dropped. "Why—
why didn't you find her another home?" I tried to keep my voice
under control. "You know as well—as I do, at those places
only puppies get adopted . . .. She'll be put down." It came out
broken. I could hardly wrap my mouth about the words.
"Oh, not at all. Pica's so adorable she's bound to find
a family that will take her in!" He shook his head
with a dismissive grin, & then went on again about the endless
pleasures of his newborn son. & I said nothing further.
What more, I'd like to know, could I have said? By the time
I was done reading it, the sun was setting. I sat there for a long
moment, then read it through a second time, trying, this time,
to be careful not to betray our friendship, to keep in mind
what a decent, fine, well-intentioned fellow he had been,
& all that he had suffered. Though it didn't work. Pica
kept pacing back and forth across the cage of that disquieting
letter, pausing now & then to lick the back of my right hand.
She could not comprehend what had happened.
Had she done something wrong? Where were those humans

she had loved so much, those humans who had seemed
so trustworthy & generous & kind? I watched through the west
window bands of violet & magenta spread across the summer
dusk & darken. I folded up his letter, set it down. But try
as I might, however much good luck I wished him in his new life,
I could not rid myself of it—that old, unspoken, unforgiving anger.

Memorial Day

Because our sons adore their plastic missile launchers,
electronic space bazookas, neutron death-ray guns,
a decade down the pike it won't prove difficult
to trick them out in combat boots
& camouflage fatigues,
rouse them with a frenzy of parades, the heady
rhetoric of country, camaraderie & God,
the drum & bugle & the sudden
thunder of the cannon as they march
into Hell singing.
Which is the order of things.
Obedient to a fault, the people will do as they are told.
However dispirited by grief at the graves
of their fallen, the mother returns at last to her loom,
the father to his lathe,
& the inconsolable widow home to raise sons
ardent for the next imperial bloodbath:
        Ilium. Thermopylae. Verdun. Pork Chop Hill.

The Grammar Lesson

for Dorianne

A noun's a thing. A verb's the thing it does.
An adjective is what describes the noun.
In "The can of beets is filled with purple fuzz,"

of and *with* are prepositions. *The*'s
an article, a *can*'s a noun.
A noun's a thing. A verb's the thing it does.

A can *can* roll—or not. What isn't was
or might be, *might* meaning not yet known.
"Our can of beets *is* filled with purple fuzz"

is present tense. While words like *our* and *us*
are pronouns—i.e., *it* is moldy, *they* are icky brown.
A noun's a thing; a verb's the thing it does.

Is is a helping verb. It helps because
filled isn't a full verb. *Can*'s what *our* owns
in "*Our* can of beets is filled with purple fuzz."

See? There's nothing to it. Just
memorize these simple rules . . . or write them down:
a noun's a thing; a verb's the thing it does.
The can of beets is filled with purple fuzz.

Little Miss Broadway

1938 & it's official—Norma Shearer will play Scarlett O'Hara.
Hit by an aerial torpedo, the freighter *Thorpeness*
burns & sinks outside Valencia Harbor.
Joe Louis takes down Max Schmelling with a ribroaster,
five lightning hooks & a right to the jaw.
The Imperial Navy moves up the Yangtze to Matang.
In Paris, Herschel Grynzpan shoots Ernst vom Rath.
The Kristallnacht Riots erupt. Superman debuts,
hoisting a green car over his head. Neville Chamberlain
signs a pact with the Reich, assuring peace
in our time. Mott's Apple Juice hits the American market.
On Thursday, June 30th, while Stéphane Grappelli
& Django Reinhardt record "Limehouse Blues"
at the Hot Club in Paris, Billie Kowit, née Ginsburg,
gives birth to a son. At Pimlico, Seabiscuit
beats War Admiral by four lengths. The Nuremberg Laws
clamp shut their teeth on the throats
of the Romani people & Jews. The exterminations begin
—Nuremberg, which gave us the clock with the toothed wheel.
David Ben-Gurion declares to the Jewish Agency Executive:
"I am in favor of compulsory transfer. I see in it
nothing immoral." In front of a wax museum statue
of Mussolini, Epiphani Dante raises a pistol to his temple
& fires. Austria joins the Reich. The Sudetenland
is annexed. Decca releases Ella Fitzgerald's *This Time
It's Real*. Shirley Temple stars in *Little Miss Broadway*.

Denis, That Photo

It's not the one of you on the steps with Andy & Robert & Phil,
the four of you mugging with macho cigars: four tough union scrappers,
or the one in the corduroy jacket & dark biker shades,
or the broodingly handsome young stud in the wool sweater,
scraggly of beard & your rock-star hair gorgeously long.
God knows who snapped it, more than a decade ago.
Or the one at the table, amused & relaxed next to Alma, who's beaming.
Not even that juicy portrait of you in your leather jacket & baseball cap
standing next to Norma Hernandez, looking so much yourself, so fully
alive that it's scary, so beguiling & scruffy, so filled with that vivid,
dashing, mischievous air you had always about you. Denis,
you're so close in that photo I think I could take one little step forward
& hug you again. But not even that one. The one that I'm talking about
is you by yourself in the desert, at sunset, in shadow. Maybe
it's east of Santee or out in the Anza Borrego. You in your jacket & jeans,
right arm extended behind you, palm open, gesturing back
toward those incandescent mauve hills, the sky a luminous blue
brushed with the purples of dusk; in the uppermost left a white cloud
fringed in *sandia* red like some kind of halo: mysterious, ethereal. You
in the quiet dark with that puckish grin: half Irish wit & half tender grace,
pleased with it all. The sweep of your arm as much as to say *Look!*
This is just what I meant. What I've been trying to say the whole time!
See, it's exactly this I've been wanting to tell you. & after it's snapped,
I can just hear that wry, ironic grunt of your satisfied, shy metaphysical
laugh. It's that one of you by yourself, in a gesture of absolute
welcome, under a sky glowing at sunset, behind you those hills & that white
oracular cloud far to your left with its rapturous halo, portent of all things
that cannot be spoken. & you, ever the urbane, gracious host. *C'mon,*
you're saying. *Let's keep on walking. We'll get even closer.* Denis, it's that one.

Denis Callahan 1957-2006

The Bridge

Climbed up past the ridge,
slipped off my pack,
& sat there
on that viewy overhang,
the emerald vista
vast & luminous
as I'd remembered.
A pair of hawks
circled slowly far below.
The world is opulent,
indifferent, undeceitful.
Still & all, its latter purposes
elude us.
Brushing away a fly
that had been buzzing
at my skull,
I dug out of my pack
a pippin apple.
At my feet, flakes of mica
glistened
in the faceted conglomerate,
& to my left, suspended
from two stalks
of mountain lilac
past their bloom,
a miniature bridge:
the swaying membrane
of a web
some solitary spider
had abandoned—
a single strand,
half glowing in the light,
& half invisible.

Days of '65

I want it back—that sixth floor walk-up
with its lilac curtains. City
full of sirens, bookshops, dim cafés.
I want the candles & the rum,
the fevered talk. A flickering of neon
thru the blinds. That bong's sweet scent

& glow. Che's photo taped
above my ancient stereo. Some angel
purring softly in the dark. A plaintive
keyboard . . . sultry horn . . . insistent drum.

Raven

Squawks from a raven in what used to be Jack
Funk's field over the fence, scolding me
till I look up & see that the hills
are still there, that the day
couldn't be lovelier, sweeter. Susan Green's
little girls are chatting in singsong
up in the tree house
in what used to be Dempsey's old place
to the west. Mary, who will stroll over these four-
point-five acres of rolling high desert chaparral
when we two are gone? The tin barn,
the pump house & shed. That underground
stream from which we've been drinking
our fill these eighteen years.
Who'll own all this dusty blue mountain lilac,
the aloe & roses & pines & bright orange iceplant?
Who'll walk in the shade of that live oak
under which Ralphie & Ivan & Charlie,
& Eddie are buried? Who'll watch the quail
flutter out of the brush in formation,
& the rabbits scurry for cover? Who
will these granite boulders & lovely agaves
belong to when you & I, beloved, are buried
& long forgotten? —Forgive me,
sweet earth, for not being shaken more often
out of the heavy sleep of the self. *Wake up!*
Wake up! scolds the raven, sailing off
over the canyon. *Wake up! Wake up!*

Kelly Park

Late fall: gray macadam Brooklyn afternoon.
The Brighton local rumbles on its trestle
over Kelly Park. We're pedaling 3-speed bikes
around the baseball field, the big kids
belting fungoes toward the fence.
This bike of mine that never had a right-hand
rubber grip, it's blue & yellow
with a rusted bell. How cold
that handlebar still feels against my palm!
Right here I lean into that bracing gust, then
turn, the wind at last behind me. Look!
This is the moment when I pick up speed.
At the crack of the bat, the ball at once
both rises toward the left field fence
& drops into a fielder's waiting glove—
all this in one swift parabolic arc. Who
could have guessed it would rush by so fast?
November. Brooklyn. 1950-something. Kelly Park.

Passing Thru

Astonishing, isn't it—all of these odd-
looking creatures darting around
in the grass—the lizards
& foraging bugs
& the ones that are nothing but specks
of color flitting about
on invisible wings,
each with its private sorrow
& pleasure, its own secret life.
How strange to be here at all
talking to you like this in a poem—
if only a moment our two psyches
touching.
Isn't it weird?
Don't you feel it too—how unspeakably
odd everything is?
Friend, walk mindfully here.
Even the least of these creatures
finds precious
beyond measure
its one brief season on Earth.

New Poems
(2015)

Raymond

Jesus comes back like he said he would, a stand-up kind of guy:
unassuming to a fault but rock-solid. The shy type everyone
likes but no one thinks much about one way or the other,
until one evening, during a storm, tooling down I-15
in his beat-up VW Bug, he passes one of those awful
two-car collisions, & pulling to the shoulder, hops out, strolls
past the paramedics & cops, & before they can think to stop him,
kneels into all that shattered glass by the gurneys & sheets
& with a few incomprehensible words in a language
nobody's spoken in two thousand years, coaxes the dead back
to life. The little kid gets back his severed leg & all that blood
on the road disappears like a bottle of trick ink. Then everyone
starts waking up. Even the drunk in the Chevy, sober
for once, & looking sheepish as hell. Thank God, he thinks,
no one was hurt. Outraged, the cops wrestle Jesus
to the mud, snap on the cuffs & toss him in the back of their
squad car. But when they're done helping the two ladies
& the kid to their feet & walk back, the cuffs are on the dashboard
& their black K-9 Lab retriever is curled in the guy's lap,
Jesus scratching the fellow behind the ears—something
no one's thought to do since he was a pup.
Listen, you know as well as I that none of this is true,
just a story I made up about the world we would like to have
been born into, that world where nothing that we love has to die.
But the Lab retriever I was thinking of was real: gone many years now,
our sweet beloved Raymond, his black bushy tail twitching happily
in his sleep, as he'd lie at the foot of our bed, the way he used to.

The Box Elder Bug

When Mary asks if the little bug that I've just carried safely out on a stick
& shaken into the garden was a box elder bug, I put down
the *Union-Trib*, clear my throat, & say in my most authoritative manner,
"It most certainly was a box elder bug." She nods in that typical
wiseass way of hers & says, "I bet you don't even know what a box elder
bug looks like," to which I reply: "the box elder, commonly referred to by
entomologists as *Leptocoris trivittatus*, is a dark brown coreid with three
longitudinal red lines on the thorax and red veins in the first pair of wings.
It feeds," I add as an afterthought, "mainly on the leaves of the silver
maple, that is to say the box elder tree. Hence its name."
Well, actually that's what I would have liked to have said, but couldn't
because in fact I had no idea whatsoever what a box elder bug looks like,
so I didn't know if the beautiful little creature standing on its elegant black legs
that I'd just saved from the sharp claws of our cat Bert was in fact a box
elder bug or not. Nor did I know the box elder bug fed on the box elder tree,
or that the box elder tree was also a silver maple, at least not until I walked
into what I would like to call my study, that shamble of books & manuscripts
where, at my old Pentium 4, I looked up "Box Elder bug" on *Britannica Online*,
& saw at once from the photo that the creature I'd taken outside was not a box
elder bug. But more importantly, just about every box elder bug website
Google comes up with refers to it as a pest, & there are all kinds of instructions
on how to exterminate it, simply because it tends to winter in human houses,
though in fact it does no damage whatsoever. The worst it can be accused of
is crapping on draperies creating tiny spots that are hard to remove.
Well, to hell with the draperies. The poor little things don't even damage the box
elder trees they like to eat from. In short that beautiful little box elder bug
is utterly harmless. If anyone's a pest for chrissake it's us, isn't it? *Homo
satanicus*—our own sanctimonious, genocidal, torture-loving,
insecticide-happy, maniacally exterminationist species, a species that—Well,
don't get me started. No, the bug I took outside & shook off that stick
wasn't a box elder, though I have no doubt whatsoever that exquisite little fellow
with his red cap & long handsome legs was every bit as benign
& seemed, as I carried him out, full of dignity & grace,
despite what must well have been his perfectly understandable fear
that he was being carried to his doom, some wretched Gaza or Auschwitz
or Nagasaki for bugs, though he is in fact far safer outside

than in a house with seven rambunctious cats, & he won't freeze this week:
it's the evening of the first full moon of spring—
& the weather has turned absolutely luscious & the mountain lilac is in bloom
& the snowy alyssum & African daisies & every which
sort of miraculous tiny vivid wildflower here in the back country hills.
I mean our job is to look after each other, isn't it, & save whomever we can.
Which is when, letting him drop gently into the grass, I look around at this world
for the first time all day: In the western sky, the darkening reds of dusk.
Tecate Peak, sacred Mt. Kachama, looming over the hills of Mexico. Then, back
in the house I sit by the fireplace beneath the photo of that old Palestinian
shoemaker that my uncle George took many years ago. On the mantel,
above my left shoulder, the Cambodian Buddha that Patrick gave me,
& on the chipped brick hearth by my left foot that little tin armadillo.
In the *Union-Trib* I am taking in the most recent horrors that our human brethren
have unleashed upon one another when Mary looks up from the book
she's been reading & asks me if the bug I just took outside was a box elder,
& I nod, as I've already told you, in my most authoritative manner, & fold
the newspaper & clear my throat, & tell her that yes, it most certainly was.

The Visit

It was late & since Mary was already asleep, I figured I'd make
another stab at cleaning that frustratingly cluttered desk
where I write my poems, before turning in for the night.
But when I whispered softly, "Honey, sleep well," certain she wouldn't
hear me, she unexpectedly opened her eyes & after a moment
by way of explaining why she was lying awake, said, in a quiet voice
weighted with grief, that last night Ivan had come back for a visit.

I nodded, mumbling something or other to let her know that
I understood, & watched as her eyes closed again & she drifted
uneasily into that world that is even stranger than this one,
that world into which those who have left us for good
sometimes return. Of course I was taken aback, given how many
years ago all of that was. Ivan, her beloved companion & solace
back in that Ebers Street place those three years I was gone—
that feisty, game, affable cat who was with us still when we
were together again, in those houses we rented in Lakeside & Santee,
& then up here in this tiny place in the hills in that final year of his life,
by then an old, scraggly tom ridden with cancer, hobbling about on three
legs. Ivan—one more small grief that the heart pretends it can bear.

I clicked off the light, letting her sleep, & walked down the hallway
into this tiny unkempt room, my so-called study, this jumble
of books & papers & half-finished poems. Yes, painful for sure,
but a gift nonetheless, a visit like that from someone
she'd loved with such unbroken devotion—Ivan, who'd managed
somehow to find his way back to this house, & to curl up beside
her again, if ever so briefly, is what I was thinking, as I sat myself
down here at this desk that I'm always planning to clean, & wrote this.

A Prayer

If it wasn't for Mary who knows all too well my oblivious nature,
I'd never have noticed those tiny, crepuscular creatures
floating around in the dogs' water bowls. The big, fat yellow
jackets are easy enough to spot & easy to save—You just
cup your hand under their bellies tossing them free with a splash
& they'll stumble back to their feet like indignant drunks, shake
out their wings, & fly off. But I'd never noticed those minuscule
midges & gnats till Mary pointed them out. At a casual glance
they are nothing but dust motes & flecks of debris.
By the time I bend over to look, a few have already been
pulled under & are hopelessly gone. But the ones still floating,
the ones still barely alive but alive nonetheless, you can lift out
on the tip of your finger, then gingerly coax onto dry cardboard
or fencing or whatever is lying around—though for god's sakes
be careful! A single slip can prove fatal. But if you're patient
& steady enough, you'll see wings, delicate as the lash of a small
child's eye, at last start to flutter. What has been saved,
though easy enough to disparage, is somebody's precious,
irreplaceable life. Given this planet's unending grief, let us
save whom we can. Eons after the last hominid skull has
crumbled back into the loam, may swarms of these all
but invisible creatures' descendants coast still, at dusk,
over these hills. May they find water & food in abundance.
May every breeze upon which they sail prove benign.

Passing the Potrero Graveyard

It isn't often I see someone in that little country graveyard
on Potrero Valley Road, but this morning as I drove past,
two women, each clutching a bouquet of flowers, were walking
toward a polished granite headstone in that solemn
& deliberate way that people walk when visiting their dead.
An hour earlier you'd left for Minneapolis. Your folks,
in their mid-eighties now, are clearly failing. When you get in,
they'll fuss & laugh: perhaps the last time in this world you'll
ever see them. I think of that baronial Jewish cemetery back
in New Jersey where my parents are laid to rest. For a moment,
driving through the Barrett Hills, I long to be there, kneeling
where they lie, to kiss their graves &, weeping, tell them that I—
well, you know the stuff that people always say, as if the dead
were lying there awake & listening. Dearest, I already miss you.
For a week I'll try to stop complaining—though it's my nature—
& make do: I'll pour birdseed in the feeders for the finches
& grosbeaks & jays, remembering how vulnerable all of us are
& how briefly everything exists. I'll feed our furry little
sweethearts & make certain Wally has his final dose of Baytril
& take Jesse for his walks—that slow, difficult circle he makes
these days around our modest property—& hide his Tramadol
& Chondroflex in glops of cream cheese, per your instructions,
& as I promised, every second day I'll water the tomatoes & the
jasmine & the bougainvillea & roses & ice plant & the crape myrtle.

Mercado

& the market, not to be missed:
At the entrance the dueña
With pocket mirrors, portraits
Of Agua Santa & busts
Of a tormented Christ
In little gold frames.
& in back
on a tray of guts
& pieces of brain,
the head of a pig,
mouth gaping,
its face fixed
In that final hideous shriek.

The Poets Are At It Again

The afternoon had been sullen with rain & for a spot of relief
from my altogether quotidian chores I had turned to a promising journal
of verse newly arrived in the mail to restore, to whatever modest degree,
my spirits, grown murky & sodden—something to kindle this world
back into wonder & grace. For me there is no art more exalted:
those ancient idylls & ballads called forth from the wellsprings
of human pathos & anguish, elegiacs to honor our dead
or conjure the incandescent raptures of longing.
Hell, to tell you the truth, I'm a bit of an amateur versifier myself,
with a poet's delight in the runic trope, the alchemical figure,
the unparaphrasable phrase.
But when I open the journal to read
in the very first poem that "the fibrillate air tracking the circles of breath
fractures the nuptual gloom to redeem the duplicitous scaffolds of time,"
I turn the page fast. & what on earth may I ask does that next poet mean
to suggest when he speaks of "Noon's quasi-harmonic unmooring"?
& how in Christ's name is it "rife with the snows of derision"? Is the flesh,
as another contends, nothing less than "lamentation's endogenous shadow"?
"The draconian wind's vestibular chant," still another informs me,
"throbs like the tongues of a city of trumpeting plectra where orphans
of imminence jangle the serpentine dust." Huh? I am frankly nonplussed.
Is there something earlier on that I'd missed? On the following page
yet another insists "one must storm the architectonics of flesh wherein
filial trust & clyptatic departures are one, lest, taking wing, we shall all
inexplicably perish." Whoa! Clyptatic departures? I set the quarterly back
on the table, face down. Happily, tucked among the day's
overdue bills & solicitations for money is one of those little stapled,
junk-mail lingerie & summer wear catalogues: Irresistible minis of cotton,
silk & chiffon, cheeky peekaboo push-ups & lacy thongs.
I lean back with a sigh in that big sling chair by the window, to relish
those lyrical, unambiguous paeans to longing & romance & fervid
enchantment & grace. Pure poetry, page after page after ravishing page.

Check the Map

Let's all take a deep breath and repeat after me:
Give war a chance. This is Afghanistan
we're talking about. Check the map. It's far away.

—Thomas Friedman, *New York Times 11/2/01*

But what if tomorrow turning the corner, it's not that familiar
street with its elegant two-story homes & luxurious lawns,
but a gutted-out havoc of empty doorframes,
& shattered remains of what once had been walls. Overhead,
the shrieks of B52s diving back thru the clouds. A smothering
haze thru which you see women in burkhas down
on their knees digging their dead from under the rubble.
Two blocks from home but it's suddenly Kandahar,
the Kapisa Valley, Mazar-i-Sharif. That wreaking
of vengeance you were so pleased to watch on TV.
But it's you now who cannot stop coughing, whose mouth
has dropped open in terror, whose eyes smart
in that acrid smoke; you who are scurrying, shuddering,
hugging the shadows. Till you manage, somehow, at last,
to find your way home: that snug little duplex
with its American flag decal stuck on the window over the door.
Still shaking, you get the key in the lock & stumble
into your favorite chair. But it's hours before your heart
stops pounding inside your chest & you're able to breathe,
till you no longer retch over the toilet, till you've got
yourself calm & all but convinced it must have
been some sort of vertigo, seizure, delirious
dream. But now—thank the good lord—you've come
to your senses at last, & are more or less clear who
you are, where you live, what it is you're supposed to believe.

Taedong River Bridge

In memory of Jerry Greenberg

Retreating, Walker's 8th Army torched whatever lay in its path,
battered Pyongyang with rockets & mortars till the whole
besieged city crumbled in flame. Blew up the granaries, too,
& the bridges & roads, so that those who didn't freeze to death
would be sure to die of starvation—vengeance against the Chinese
Red Army & the peasant armies of North Korea for beating them
back to Inchon. The U.S. command shelling that city till nothing
remained but that one standing bridge: tangle of girders with hardly
a place to find footing & nothing to hold as it swayed in the sleet
& the wind over those waters—Taedong River Bridge, the only
way left, short of death, to cross out of Pyongyang. Ten
thousand terrified souls swarming over its splintered ribs.
On their backs, in their arms, whatever they owned or could carry.
Women cradled their infants. Men strapped what they could
to their shoulders. The crippled & dying & blind inching their way,
for to slip—& hundreds of those fleeing slipped—was to vanish
into the icy hell of that river. Then the others would clutch one another
& wail in that other language of theirs, while they kept moving.
What else could they do? For what it was worth, those
who fell through saved the lives of those inching behind them,
letting them know where not to step next.
                                        Jerry,
that's what you did for me, too. Now & again, that awful black limo
pulls up at the curb in front of our house back in Flatbush,
& Henrietta, your mother, steps out, gaunt as death in that black
cotton shawl while I watch from an upstairs window. At which moment
my own beloved mother slips into the room, lays a hand on my shoulder,
& tells me, quietly, lest I say the wrong thing when her dearest friend
enters the house, what she had hoped never to have to tell me at all:
that you had been killed at the front. I was twelve. Forty years later
I remain stunned. Now & again, something triggers it back & I drift out
to Kelly Park & watch you fast-break down court—that long,
floating jump from the corner. The swish of the net.

Jerry, I don't know you'd care,
but when my number came up for the next imperial bloodbath
I gave my draft board the finger—for us both. And for every last
terrified soul on both sides. I can't tell you how grieved I am still
that you're gone. Or thank you enough for the warning: your death
letting me know where I stand, who my real enemies are,
what the heavy money had in store for me too.
In a way, then, I owe you my life: more than anyone else, you
were the one who showed me where not to step next
— the one up ahead, in the bitter wind of the past, who fell through.

Leah's Daughter

The workshop was just about to get started when somebody noticed
that Leah looked glum & distracted & asked what was wrong,
& Leah told us her daughter had called from Iraq that morning,
hysterical, screaming & weeping. Trained as an army clerk,
she'd been reassigned & was driving sniper patrols around
in a Humvee. The afternoon of the day before, they'd spied two
guys at the side of a road wiring an IED, & behind them, sitting
& playing, were two little kids. "Mom," Leah said her daughter
kept screaming into the phone, "my guys fired round after round
after round till the four were nothing but torn open bodies
& heads without faces in puddles of blood & my guys just kept
laughing & shooting & laughing & shooting & Mom, they
were just little kids! Oh my god," she kept crying, "It's not right!
It just isn't right!" We sat there, all of us, horrified, silent.
Till finally, Karen said, "That's awful, Leah!" & after a minute or two,
when no one said anything more, I started taking attendance.
Then we critiqued the first poem: an honest, if somewhat
disorganized story of failed love. But of course it was still
on everyone's mind, & someone, I think it was Teri, asked Leah
how old her daughter was & how long before she'd
get to come home. "It's her second deploy," Leah said quietly.
"She'll be twenty in August. She's got four months & six days
to go if her tour isn't extended like last time & if . . . ." She stopped,
mid-sentence. No one said anything further. Like everyone
else, I kept my mouth shut, & we moved on to the next poem.

A Note Concerning My Military Career

After I'd sent the army my letter of resignation, two beefy Intelligence types
showed up at my place in the Fillmore with a huge reel-to-reel tape recorder,
& without mincing words I tore into America's bloodthirsty agenda:
the circle of hell reserved for the savage carpet bombing campaign
against the people of Vietnam, & the puppet state that the U.S. was trying
to force down their throats. Which was why, I explained, I wouldn't put
their fucking uniform on ever again & why, if I had to fight, it would be
for the other side.
   Quiet, courteous, polite, they sat there for two hours
listening to my ferocious rant till I asked what exactly it was they needed
to know, & one of them said they had really been sent to find out if I
was planning to shoot President Johnson, or do something else of that sort,
& I laughed & said no, & we shook hands & they packed up & left.
But a month later, when the army sent me the transcript to sign & return,
I brought it instead to a young San Francisco attorney whose family firm
did *pro bono* work for resisters, & Butch Hallinan read that whole eighteen-
page harangue & looked up & told me how much he liked what I'd said,
& when I asked him what to do next, he advised me to get the hell out of town
as fast as I could. Which I did. I ran for my life & for the lives of all those
they were trying to get me to kill, & of nothing I've done in this world
have I ever been prouder.
   Listen, if you're reading this poem & you're young
or desperate enough to think of enlisting, or have already been suckered in,
understand that despite all those self-righteous fairy tales about freedom
& peace, this nation has been from its genocidal beginnings addicted
to empire, plunder & perpetual war. Those combat flicks you watched as a kid,
& the sanctimonious propaganda that passes for news, & the swaggering,
hawkish prattle puked from the lips of our politicians & pundits—that spew
stinking of corpses & money—are meant to convince young men
& women like you to massacre, city by city & village by village,
America's villain *du jour*, adding, every few years, another small state
that stepped out of line to its necklace of skulls.
& for those of you who will march to your own graves in so doing,
the powers that sent you will bow their heads & present to your folks
the flag that was draped on the box they carted you home in.
   Friend, find any way that you can to resist
or escape. If you have to run for your life, for chrissake, run for your life.

Three Gents

For Al Zolynas & in memory of Fred Moramarco

We've been strolling down the beach, three elder gents,
discussing matters subtle & abstruse, as is our wont:
Occam's Razor, Zeno's paradox, the Nimzo-Indian Defense.

While twenty-somethings jog & swim, toss frisbees, crest
the breakers on their longboards, shmooze or flaunt
their pecs & abs & legs & lovely breasts, we gents

with roving eyes are parsing out the elements
of Rational Decision Theory, Pascal's Triangle, the daunt-
ing issue of the cubic & the Nimzo-Indian Defense.

O rapture of beguiling flesh! Whither? Whence?
The Prisoner's Dilemma, Drake's Equation, Hume or Kant:
That redhead in her string bikini thong. Three anadipsic gents

guzzling down Foucault, ontogeny, unknowable events,
antimatter, counterfactuals, the permutations of Necessity & Want,
these grains of sand, uncountable, the ontological significance

of Fibonacci numbers, breasting waves, time's sting, the dance
of Eros, chance, Pyrronian regress. Pierced by its pointed horns, this Body-Mind Dilemma. Lost, three elder gents,
in dreams, the carnal itch, the Nimzo-Indian Defense.

Some Marionettes

One afternoon, years back, in a distant city, I found myself staring
into the window display of a toy store that some ingenious window
designer & puppet-maker had fashioned of cardboard and papier maché
& painted to look like the very street I was on: its small luncheonette
& canopied shops a perfect replica, down to this very toy store itself,
& out on the sidewalk, puppets jerking about on their shiny black strings
like frenzied pedestrians racing in every direction. A couple with
gift-wrapped boxes in both hands was stepping out of a doorway;
there were elderly gents & lady puppets in high-fashion furs, sailors
in white caps, a merchant in front of his shop stroking his mustache,
a girl in red pumps, a kid on a bike & two on skateboards,
businessmen clutching their attaché cases, a dowager walking
three Pekingese, a small boy being pulled along by his mother,
hardhats in t-shirts drilling into a cordoned-off piece of the roadway,
the whole macaronic parade of them bouncing in place
in that urgent, convulsive way puppets do: & none of them, needless
to say, making the least bit of headway. The whole thing at once
striking & comic, but somehow mysterious, too, & inexplicably touching.
I stood there a long while—amused, appalled & entranced,
till I came to myself & saw with a glance at my watch how much later
it was than I'd thought, & with that I rushed off down that street
with its chaos of scurrying figures—that blur of dizzying shadows—myself,
once again, intent on whatever urgent errand it was that had brought me.

Progeria

Those kids who age prematurely:
at seven already sclerotic & grey.
& I too! Though at first glance
I seem a man long past his youth,
just a day or two back I was a boy
tossing a softball out in the school yard.
This wretched, incurable curse!
One moment of sheer exuberant joy
& the next you're bent, deaf, gasping
for breath, your flesh splotched,
& hands that never stop shaking.

I Stand in the Doorway

Sometimes when you say goodbye you know it's goodbye for keeps.
You touch your lips to her cheek, or you squeeze his hand & walk off.
What else can you do? Out on the street, the light has never
been so intense, luminous, intolerably bright.
But mostly we don't know when it's that last hug, the final goodbye.
Who would have guessed that perfectly casual "Hey, Steve, take care,"
was the last. Years later someone mentions that Greg's living
somewhere in Spain or Rebecca got married in Quito. Don,
someone says, is in Shreveport. Or you hear through the grapevine
that Kenny has died, someone you once loved, someone with whom
you spent endless hours laughing back in those feverish days
on that other coast, in that other life. One morning you turn
the page of the *Union-Trib* & among the obits there's a picture of Larry,
from the old coalition, & you read that small notice beneath it
& your heart stops dead in its tracks. One afternoon,
at Dennis's bookshop up on Girard some guy you don't quite remember
starts shaking your hand & tells you that Susan died of stomach
cancer five years ago now. "I wasn't sure that you knew." & in fact
you didn't know. & Elliot Berke, swallowed by time. Was that the last
goodbye, there in the narrow hallway of that 6th floor walk-up of mine,
all those decades ago? Elliot grinning that edgy, cherubic grin & turning
to leave, & me with my hand on the tarnished knob of that door watching
him make his way down the stairs in the dusty, fluorescent semi-dark
of that place fifty years back, that door which hasn't yet quite shut for good.

Cherish

"We are not interested in the poetry of nostalgia."
—submission guidelines for a literary journal

Yes, of course, the sign & the thing-in-itself are in no manner
the same. It goes without saying. We all understand the grammatological
nature of meta-phonemic & proto-factual discourse: what Troubetzkoy
would surely have called the contingent glossomatics
of the indeterminate text. But the trouble is, notwithstanding all that,
the past won't shut up. Won't leave me in peace. I want it all back.
Not the nomenclature of epistemic linguistics or some sort of post-dialectic
mode of discursive assertion, but rather my folks in that cozy doorway
in Flatbush, that house on 14th Street, Carol's old piano,
Mickey's black, wooden *Attorney at Law* sign hung from the window
over that shingled hatch to the basement. & that little storefront
on 10th, where I hawked Circle Line tours of Manhattan. My booth
at the Magic Carpet, just off the boardwalk, in Coney Island, three
blocks from Nathan's, the North Atlantic pounding away at my back.
That movie house in Miami where the black patrons had to sit
in the balcony: I could hardly fucking believe it, & worked there with a bad
conscience for two months.
       Would they have me abandon the past?
Devote what time I have left to the unstable nature of syntax?
the manipulation of self-referential lexical signs? I, the most shameless
& least enigmatic of singers? I, who wish no more
than to remember & cherish. I, who now to my own grief understand well,
in the words of Nicanor Parra, that the decades have wings.
Despite the indeterminate, self-defeating problematics of verbal
representation, I insist that furnished place up on 92nd, off Amsterdam
Avenue, really exists . . . or it did, & those evenings spent haunting
the Thalia: those ancient, grainy Chaplin & Marx Brothers slapsticks.
& that woman I brought home one night from the Cedar, where Franz
Kline used to hold court; not a "structural coefficient of syntactic presence,"
but an actual woman, George Antheil's old flame. & the evening
I spent there with Duncan, & the week Jim Fraser came back
from his pilgrimage to the Scottish highlands, sporting kilts,
& he & I took that place together off Avenue B, where Carol Berge
lived with Peter, & Sandra Scoppettone had a place

just down the hall, *Suzuki Beane* already a raging success,
& a flight above me, Bill Merwin & Moira. One morning, trembling,
I sat on a bench in Tompkins Square Park ingesting that first
City Lights edition of *Howl*, that ferocious, tidal American rant
— like those earlier days when I'd ride the Brighton Express
reading Whitman & weeping. It was Allen himself one night
after a reading at St. Marks a good decade later who introduced
me to Parra, whom he knew I adored, & I stood there
stupidly shaking his hand with nothing to say.
                              To hell
with the signifier's oblique figurations, the *nomos* of indeterminate
linguistic praxis. It's those mornings waking with Rozzie, my first love,
back there on 6th Street, the past even now inexpressibly present.
The evening that Jane & Wendy dragged me to Gerde's Folk City
to watch some kid named Dylan wailing over the mike: Diane,
this time around I'll let you do that striptease at the party, why
the hell not. Then we'll head back to my place. No, this time
I'm not gonna stop you. Nor do I mean to ever forget your sister
dying like that, so suddenly, so young. Cassidy too, gone now forever,
& Joan & Linda, & Jeremy, Jon, Federico, Denis & Greg, & Mickey
& Doug, & that large, loving boisterous tribe of aunts & uncles
& cousins: Sally & Gertie & Manus & Mark & Al & Lily & George
& Terry & Molly & Willy & Nat.
                              I want to be there again. Those teeming
streets of downtown Manhattan, those Lower East Side cafés
—all those poets & dopers & crazies back in the '60s. The friends
that I'll never now get to cherish enough: Allen Cohen & Faye Goldman
& lovely, voluptuous Billie Grayson out on the Tilden clay courts.
Is Eddie De Marco alive? Is Vinnie? Lou Lipton? Marilyn Branscomb?
Cherish! Cherish! That's all I can tell you. Sign & signifier be damned!
No one & nothing down here is going to last! You know it, too. Nicanor
Parra—wasn't he right on the money? Though the days drag their
feet, & the weeks creep ever so slowly along, the decades have wings.

202 East 7th

Now & again I catch myself staring back
into that world, decades gone. Cassidy
is defending the Chinese Revolution, arms
crossed over his lean, naked chest.
He is 20, agitated of course, but laughing
nevertheless as he paces the room.
From a chair in the corner, Doug Reisner's
hoarse, equivocal chuckle, & Lenny
is grinning, delighted, & Murray, laconic
as ever, nodding his head. That quiet,
measured womanly voice is Susan
Hartung's. Outside, the blazing white
impossible glare from the street, & more
dimly lit than I guess it must really have
been, the narrow, endless tenement
stairway I climb to that earlier life,
in this waking dream, again & again.

Yes, Indeed!

Now that it's done,
what's left
but to grin inanely
bobbing my head
in maniacal glee
& licking
my upper lip
with my tongue
again & again
while jotting it down,
or as much as I dare to,
& as fast as I can.

Acknowledgments

I am grateful to the publishers of the following books in which some of these poems were published:

Carpenter Press, which published the collection *Lurid Confessions* in 1983, a book reprinted by Serving House Books in 2010.

The Roundhouse Press, Heyday Books, which published *The Dumbbell Nebula* in 2000.

The University of Tampa Press, which published *The First Noble Truth* in 2007.

For first publication of some of the "New Poems" in this collection, the author also wishes to acknowledge the following presses and journals:

Spuyten Duyvil Press, which published "Check the Map" and "Taedong River Bridge" in *Crossing Borders*, an art/poetry book with eight poems by Steve Kowit and drawings and paintings by Lenny Silverberg, in 2010.

Poetry International, which published "The Box Elder Bug."

The Passaic Review, which published "The Poets Are At It Again."

The Sun, which published "A Betrayal," "After Surgery," "A Note Concerning My Military Career," "A Prayer," "I Stand in the Doorway," "Leah's Daughter," "Passing the Potrero Graveyard," "Progeria," "Raymond," "Some Marionettes," "Taedong River Bridge," "The First Noble Truth," "The Visit," and "Will Boland & I."

California Journal of Poetics, which published "202 East 7th Street."

San Diego Poetry Annual, which published "Cherish."

About the Author and Artist

Steve Kowit was a California author with many collections of poetry in print, including *The Dumbbell Nebula* (Heyday Books); *The Gods of Rapture* (City Works Press), a collection of poems inspired by the erotic verse of India; *Lurid Confessions* (Serving House Press); *Crossing Borders* (Spuyten Duyvil), an art/poetry collaboration with the painter Lenny Silverberg; and *The First Noble Truth* (University of Tampa Press), winner of the Tampa Review Prize for Poetry. His work has been widely published in magazines and journals and has been read by Garrison Keillor on National Public Radio. His teaching manual, *In the Palm of Your Hand: The Poet's Portable Workshop* (Tilbury House), is widely used by writing groups, workshops, and individual writers throughout the country. He was the recipient of a National Endowment Fellowship in Poetry, two Pushcart Prizes, and numerous other awards.

Kowit grew up in New York and then spent a few years in San Francisco during that city's brief counterculture revolution. After refusing to serve in Vietnam, he spent three years living in Mexico, Central America, and South America. Returning to the U.S., he worked as a book editor in Florida and then moved to San Diego, where he founded that city's first animal rights organization and became involved in the Zen, Vipassana, and Gurdjieff communities.

He taught at colleges in Idaho and Maryland and in California at the University of California, San Diego; San Diego State University; and Southwestern College. Until his death on April 2, 2015, he lived in the back-country hills of San Diego county near the Tecate border with his wife Mary and several animal companions.

Joel Kowit is Professor of Biology at Emmanuel College, Boston, where he has taught for thirty-eight years. He serves as a consultant in immunology for numerous pharmaceutical companies and has also been a graphic artist for the past thirty years, producing numerous scientific illustrations for Immunology Workshops (www.immunologyworkshops.com). His solo exhibitions include shows at the Cary Library, Lexington, at "Gallery 5" at Emmanuel College, and at the Massachusetts State House, Revenue Office. His painting, "Mooring," which is featured on the cover, won Special Recognition in the 2013 "City-Scapes" Competition of the online gallery, Light Space & Time.

About the Book

Cherish is set in Adobe Garamond Pro, a digital font developed from the sixteenth century roman types of Claude Garamond and the italics of Robert Granjon. Adobe Systems type designer Robert Slimbach visited the Plantin-Moretus Museum in Antwerp, Belgium, for research while working on the font. He later wrote, "The experience of studying near flawless proofs of Garamond's and Granjon's types was a revelation which led to a major overhaul of the working design." Slimbach's original digital fonts, released in 1989, have been further refined with digital options available in the newer Open Type format. The result is a versatile and highly readable serif face that preserves the grace and proportion of classical letterforms while projecting a timeless and contemporary clarity. The book was designed and typeset by Richard Mathews at the University of Tampa Press.